ProMgmt.

K LOAN

Purchasing: Selection and Procurement for the Hospitality Industry

SIXTH EDITION

udent Workbook

National Restaurant Association
EDUCATIONAL FOUNDATION

D1341463

LEY & SONS, INC.

This student workbook is designed to be used with the textbook *Purchasing: Selection and Procurement for the Hospitality Industry, Sixth Edition* by Andrew Hale Feinstein and John Stefanelli,.

This book is printed on acid-free paper. ∞

Published by John Wiley & Sons, Inc., Hoboken, New Jersey

Published simultaneously in Canada.

This publication is designed to provide accurate and authoritative information in regard to the subject matter covered. It is sold with the understanding that the publisher is not engaged in rendering professional services. If professional advice or other expert assistance is required, the services of a competent professional should be sought.

Library of Congress Cataloging-in-Publication Data:

ISBN: 0-471-69314-6

Printed in the United States of America

10 9 8 7 6 5 4 3 2 1

CONTENTS

INTRODUCTION

Purchasing is a bottom-line concern to managers who wish to keep profit margins up, prices in line and competitive, and expenses down. The purpose of *Purchasing: Selection and Procurement for the Hospitality Industry, Sixth Edition* is to provide you with the management information needed to make purchasing decisions based on sound criteria.

This course begins with an overview of the purchasing function, and then discusses planning for purchasing. The course then looks at ordering, receiving, and storing purchases, and using computers in the purchasing function. The course covers purchasing produce, processed foods, dairy products, eggs, poultry, fish, meat, beverages, services, equipment, and finally, other nonfood items.

The ProMgmt.® Program

How to Earn a ProMgmt. Certificate of Course Completion

To earn a ProMgmt. Certificate of Course Completion, a student must complete all student workbook exercises and receive a passing score on the final examination.

Each student who submits an examination answer sheet to the NRAEF will receive a student number. Please make a record of it; this number will identify you during your present and future coursework with the NRAEF.

ProMgmt. certificate requirements are administered exclusively through colleges and other educational institutions that offer ProMgmt. courses and examinations.

If you are not currently enrolled in a ProMgmt. course and would like to earn a ProMgmt. certificate, please contact your local educational institution to see if they are willing to administer the ProMgmt. certificate requirements for non-enrolled students. You can also visit www.nraef.org for a list of ProMgmt. Partner schools. ProMgmt. Partner schools offer seven or more courses that include administration of the ProMgmt. certificate requirements.

The NRAEF leaves it to the discretion of each educational institution offering ProMgmt. courses to decide whether or not that institution will administer the ProMgmt. certificate requirements to non-enrolled students. If an institution does administer ProMgmt. certificate requirements to non-enrolled students, that institution may charge an additional fee, of an amount determined by that institution, for the administration of the ProMgmt. certificate requirements.

Course Materials

This course consists of the text, *Purchasing: Selection and Procurement for the Hospitality Industry, Sixth Edition* by Andrew Hale Feinstein and John Stefanelli; the student workbook, and a final examination. The examination is the final section of your course and is sent to an instructor for administration, then returned to the NRAEF for grading.

Each chapter consists of:

- Learning Objectives
- Chapter Study Outline
- Chapter Check-in
- Answers to Chapter Check-in (at the end of the workbook)

At the end of the workbook you will find:

- An 80-question practice test
- Answers to the practice test

The objectives indicate what you can expect to learn from the course, and are designed to help you organize your studying and concentrate on important topics and explanations. Refer to the objectives frequently to make sure you are meeting them.

The exercises help you check how well you've learned the concepts in each chapter. These will be graded by your instructor.

An 80-question Practice Test appears at the end of the workbook. All the questions are multiple-choice and have four possible answers. Circle the best answer to each question, as in this example:

Who was the first president of the United States?
A.   Thomas Jefferson
B.   *George Washington*
C.   Benjamin Franklin
D.   John Adams

Answers to the Practice Test follow in the workbook so that you can grade your own work.

The Final Exam

All examinations can first be graded by your instructor and then officially graded again by the NRAEF. If you do not receive a passing grade on the examination, you may request a retest. A retest fee will be charged for the second examination.

Study Tips

Since you have already demonstrated an interest in furthering your foodservice education by registering for this NRAEF course, you know that your next step is study preparation. We have included some specific study aids that you might find useful.

- Build studying time into your routine. If you hold a full-time job, you need to take a realistic approach to studying. Set aside a specific time and place to study, and stick to your routine as closely as possible. Your study area should have room for your course materials and any other necessary study aids. If possible, your area should be away from family traffic.
- Discuss with family members your study goals and your need for a quiet place and private time to work. They might want to help you draw up a study schedule that will be satisfactory to everyone.
- Keep a study log. You can record what chapter was worked on, a list of topics studied, the time you put in, and how well you scored on the Chapter Check-ins and Practice Text.
- Work at your own pace, but move ahead steadily. The following tips should help you get the most value from your lessons.
    1. Look over the objectives carefully. They list what you are expected to know for the examination.
    2. Read the chapters carefully, and don't hesitate to mark your text—it will help you later. Mark passages that seem especially important and those that seem difficult, as you might want to reread them later.
    3. Try to read an entire chapter at a time. Even though more than one chapter might be assigned at time, you might find you can carefully read only one chapter in a sitting.
    4. When you have finished reading the chapter, go back and check the highlights and any notes you have made. These will help you review for the examination.

Reviewing for the Final Exam

Once you have completed the final exercise and Practice Test, you will have several items to use for your examination review. If you have highlighted important points in the textbook, you can review them. If you have made notes in the margins, check them to be sure you have answered any questions that arose when you read the material. Reread certain sections if necessary. Finally, you should go over your exercises.

The ProMgmt.® Program

The National Restaurant Association Educational Foundation's ProMgmt. program is designed to provide foodservice students and professionals with a solid foundation of practical knowledge and information. Each course focuses on a specific management area. Students who earn ProMgmt. certificates improve their chances of:
- Earning NRAEF Undergraduate Scholarships.
- Gaining management jobs within the foodservice and restaurant industry.

For more information on both the ProMgmt. program and scholarships, please contact the NRAEF at 800.765.2122 (312.715.1010 in Chicagoland), or visit our Web site at **www.nraef.org**.

CHAPTER 1

THE CONCEPTS OF SELECTION AND PROCUREMENT

Learning Objectives

After reading this chapter, you should be able to:

1.1   Define the terms purchasing, selection, and procurement.

1.2   Explain how technology and e-commerce applications are changing the purchasing process in the hospitality industry.

1.3   Identify commercial and noncommercial hospitality operations.

Chapter 1 Study Outline

1. Though the term "**purchasing**" is widely used, its meaning is too restrictive; terms like "**selection**" and "**procurement**" refer to the broader buying function that occurs in hospitality operations.
    *   "**Selection**" refers to choosing among various alternatives, whereas "**procurement**" describes an orderly, systematic exchange between the buyer and seller that encompasses all the activities associated with buying, receiving, and storing products and services.

2. Technology via the Internet has revolutionized how buyers and suppliers procure products and services.
    *   **E-commerce** refers to transactions done electronically: **B2B e-commerce** refers to business-to-business electronic transactions, while **B2C e-commerce** refers to business-to-consumer electronic transactions.

3. Hospitality operations are usually divided into the commercial, institutional, and military segments.

4. The purchasing function differs according to the type of hospitality operation.
    *   Owners/managers generally do the buying for smaller, independent operations.
    *   In medium-sized, independent operations, general managers coordinate the actual buying activities with department heads.
    *   Large, independent operations often employ a full-time buyer.
    *   Multiunit companies and franchises frequently maintain central commissaries or distribution warehouses.

5. E-commerce has allowed smaller, independent hospitality operations to combine their procurement resources in a process called **co-op buying**.

- In co-op buying, independent operations enroll with an aggregate purchasing company, or "Group Purchasing Organization" (GPO), by paying a participation fee.
- In turn, GPOs use their collective buying power to negotiate competitive pricing with distributors and suppliers. The savings subsequently pass onto the independent operations that have enrolled with the GPO.

Chapter 1 Exercises

1. Indicate whether each of the following defines selection (S) or procurement (P).

_____a.   Ordering the correct amounts of products or services at the appropriate times in a timely manner

_____b.   Choosing from various alternatives on various levels

_____c.   Deciding on a particular poultry supplier

_____d.   Orderly, systematic exchange between buyer and seller

_____e.   "Nuts and bolts" of the buyer's job

L.O. 1.1

2. Identify whether each of the following is a commercial hospitality operation (C) or a noncommercial hospitality operation (N).

_____a.	Lodge		_____f.	Shelter
_____b.	University food service		_____g.	Tavern
_____c.	Camp		_____h.	Adult community
_____d.	Spa		_____i.	Military installation
_____e.	Cafeteria		_____j.	Buffet

L.O. 1.3

3. How has co-op buying been affected by e-commerce?

_____

_____

_____

L.O. 1.2

2

4. Match the operation type on the left with the purchasing process it would most likely use on the right.

_____a. Co-op of large independents

_____b. Large independent

_____c. Multi-unit chain

_____d. Franchise

_____e. Small or medium independent

1) Manager purchases some supplies from a central commissary and other supplies from local vendors.
2) Several full-time buyers make purchases together to keep costs down.
3) Owner/manager either performs or oversees all buying, receiving, storing, and issuing functions.
4) Vice president of purchasing oversees the buying and shipping of all supplies to individual units.
5) Full-time buyer purchases all supplies and distributes them to the appropriate departments.

L.O. 1.3

Chapter 1 Check-in

1. Choosing from various alternatives on various levels is known as

   A. purchasing.
   B. selection.
   C. procurement.
   D. buying.

   L.O. 1.1

2. An orderly, systematic exchange between seller and buyer is referred to as

   A. purchasing.
   B. selection.
   C. procurement.
   D. buying.

   L.O. 1.1

3. Few hospitality operations have which of the following?

   A. Quality control programs
   B. E-commerce applications
   C. Full-time buyers
   D. Opportunities for co-op purchasing

   L.O. 1.3

4. Which of the following have revolutionized the way buyers and suppliers purchase products and services?

   A. Technology-driven procurement applications
   B. Franchise opportunities
   C. REITs
   D. Commissaries

   L.O. 1.2

5. Which of the following hospitality operations is considered noncommercial?

    A. Vending machine company
    B. Food court
    C. Casino
    D. Employee feeding operation

L.O. 1.3

6. Cruise ships and airlines fall under which commercial operation category?

    A. Off-premise caterers
    B. On-premise caterers
    C. In-transit food services
    D. Transportation food services

L.O. 1.3

7. Contract foodservice companies typically operate in

    A. daycare facilities.
    B. department stores.
    C. supermarkets.
    D. banquet halls.

L.O. 1.3

8. Which of the following is an example of a self-operated community center?

    A. Military installation
    B. Correctional facility
    C. Religious facility
    D. Senior center

L.O. 1.3

9. Smaller hospitality companies can procure products at competitive prices and compete for pricing through the use of

    A. e-commerce co-op buying.
    B. aggregate purchasing.
    C. affirmative selection.
    D. universal platforms.

L.O. 1.2

10. Aggregate purchasing companies do which of the following?

    A. Buy and sell products
    B. Negotiate contracts on behalf of independent hotels, management companies, resorts, and REITs
    C. Purchase supplies primarily through a central commissary
    D. Publish electronic purchasing guides

L.O. 1.2

CHAPTER 2

TECHNOLOGY APPLICATIONS IN PURCHASING

Learning Objectives

After reading this chapter, you should be able to:

2.1   Explain how technologies are used by hospitality operators in the selection, procurement, and inventory processes.

2.2   Discuss the challenges of incorporating e-procurement strategies in the hospitality industry.

Chapter 2 Study Outline

1. Distributors use computer software applications to build customer databases, to forecast future customer growth, to create Internet-based ordering systems, and to create the most efficient delivery of goods and services.

    *   All of these programs are designed to cohesively minimize order-placing and delivery costs in order to increase margins and profitability over time.

2. Buyers use a variety of electronic equipment to enhance the purchasing function and the overall inventory control process, including fax machines, personal computers, point-of-sale systems, and bar-code readers.

    *   While fax machines may one day be replaced by e-procurement as the primary technology for ordering items, they are still widely used by buyers to submit written orders over telephone lines.

    *   Personal computers are the most powerful tool that a hospitality owner-manager can have, not only in their ability to provide a connection to other units and the Internet, but also for their ability to run sophisticated spreadsheet software.

    *   With point-of-sale or POS systems, employees use touch-screen or wireless ordering systems to electronically take and communicate a customer's order to kitchen and bar staff. When linked to an operation's main server, many POS systems can take a customer's order and incorporate it into the operation's inventory-tracking system, or even use the customer's order to trigger automated purchasing with distributors.

    *   Bar-code readers streamline the inventory-control process of a hospitality unit, and can be especially crucial in providing more accurate cost control for the beverage area. Most bar codes are based on the Universal Product Code (UPC) standard.

3. Computer technology applications help buyers prepare specifications, order products, and track inventory.

- Many guides designed to help buyers 'spec out' products are now available in CD-ROM form. These digital resources often include valuable information about the many distributors of any given product.

- E-procurement streamlines the order-taking process for both the buyer and distributor. Such e-marketplaces also often allow buyers and distributors to negotiate contractual pricing agreements prior to ordering.

- Inventory-tracking software aids hospitality operators in their cost-control efforts. Operators can choose between generic spreadsheet software, off-the-shelf software designed for the hospitality market, or original software created by software consulting firms.

4. The Internet allows buyers and suppliers to communicate easily and quickly through e-mail, newsgroups, and the World Wide Web.

- E-mail is a quick and efficient technology for communicating with both employees and outside suppliers. The technology allows users to attach documents that previously would have been sent by postal mail instantly.

- Newsgroups are electronic bulletin boards that allow people with similar interests to learn from one another's experiences. Typically, people ask questions of the group and then receive a variety of responses from the group's members. Newsgroups can provide hospitality operators with valuable information from their industry colleagues.

- The World Wide Web, or Web, is a graphical interface commonly used on the Internet to provide information to people on almost every topic imaginable. By using Internet-based search engines designed to locate information based on key words, hospitality operators can click quickly onto a "website." Once inside a site, operators can collect valuable information that's been posted to the site by a company or organization.

5. The adoption of e-procurement technologies has been challenged in recent years by reluctance on the part of employees, suppliers, and organizations.

- Employees can resist change for a variety of reasons: they may fear losing the perceived power that their knowledge of the old system provides them; they may fear that changing their work routine will negatively impact their job performance; or they may fear that technology is too quickly overtaking their lives, a phenomenon known as "future shock."

- Suppliers' fear of disintermediation (in which they are shut out of the supply chain as operators buy directly from growers and manufacturers) and an unwillingness to invest in new technologies are the main reasons suppliers are still reluctant to implement e-procurement.

- At the organizational level, difficulties in implementing industry-wide identification standards on commercial foodservice products, reluctance to do business with new, third-party dot.com companies, and a fear of depersonalization in the process all hinder the quick adoption of e-procurement.

- Steps that can be taken to increase the pace of e-procurement adoption include: better communication about the benefits of e-procurement with employees asked to implement it; a recognition by suppliers that keeping up with the needs of their customers requires them to obtain better technology; and the implementation of identification standards at the organizational level.

Chapter 2 Exercises

1. Name three ways that distributors use software applications to enhance their operations.

- _____

- _____

- _____

L.O. 2.1

2. Indicate whether each of the following relates to the fax machine (F), personal computer (PC), POS system (POS), or bar-code reader (BC).

_____a. Allows buyers to submit written orders over the telephone lines instantaneously

_____b. Streamlines the inventory-control process

_____c. Most powerful electronic tool a hospitality manager can have

_____d. Used to conduct a physical-inventory count by scanning each product in the storeroom

_____e. Contains built-in microprocessors that can tabulate and organize huge amounts of sales data quickly

_____f. Provides cost control in the beverage area by highlighting discrepancies between the amount of beverage a POS system indicates should have been used and the actual usage computed

_____g. Features touch-screen technology

_____h. First used in the 1980s to reduce the confusion and mistakes sometimes associated with verbal orders

_____i. Can stand alone or connect to other hospitality units or the Internet

_____j. Allows servers to carry a wireless ordering system from table to table

L.O. 2.1

3. Describe the product-ordering process via the e-marketplace.

_____

_____

_____

L.O. 2.1

4. Name one way that each of the following Internet features can help hospitality operators select and procure products.

   a. E-mail

   _____

   b. Newsgroups

   _____

   c. World Wide Web

   _____

L.O. 2.1

5. Briefly describe why a fear of distintermediation might cause some suppliers to hold off pursing e-procurement technologies.

_____

_____

_____

L.O. 2.2

Chapter 2 Check-in

1. Although the traditional method of verbal orders is still widely used in the hospitality industry, many buyers now use which of the following to communicate instead of the telephone?

    A. Uniform resource locator
    B. Order modifier
    C. Fax machine
    D. Hyperlink

    L.O. 2.1

2. A logistics software application that outlines routing sequences can help a supplier do which of the following?

    A. Determine the optimal number of delivery trucks to use
    B. Receive instant feedback on product pricing and availability
    C. Estimate driver downtime
    D. Streamline the inventory-control process

    L.O. 2.1

3. What is the most powerful and useful technology tool a hospitality owner/manager can have?

    A. Fax machine
    B. Point-of-sale system
    C. Bar-code reader
    D. Personal computer

    L.O. 2.1

4. Most advanced POS systems feature which of the following?

    A. Bar-code labels
    B. Touch-screen technology
    C. Wireless ordering system
    D. Inventory nodes

    L.O. 2.1

5. Which is the most common standard used for bar-code labeling systems?

    A. EAN
    B. Codabar
    C. Code 128
    D. Universal product code (UPC)

    L.O. 2.1

6. How might a buyer benefit by ordering products directly with a personal computer?

    A. Decreases the likelihood that the buyer will become a "prime vendor" account
    B. Saves time
    C. Increases labor costs
    D. Provides automatic access to competitors' specifications

    L.O. 2.1

7. In addition to an e-marketplace's ability to streamline the ordering process, it also can allow buyers to

    A. negotiate contractual pricing agreements with distributors prior to ordering.
    B. implement industry-wide identification standards.
    C. learn more about a company's founders.
    D. replace goods based on physical inventories.

    L.O. 2.1

8. An owner/operator who wanted to quickly develop strategies for reducing produce waste might want to

   A. e-mail his or her produce supplier.
   B. conduct tests on how well various produce lasts without refrigeration.
   C. post questions on a hospitality operator's newsgroup.
   D. read through a USDA guidebook.

   L.O. 2.1

9. All of the following are slowing down the pace of e-procurement *except:*

   A. Suppliers are nervous that they will be cut out of the supply chain.
   B. The industry-wide adoption of identification standards took place too quickly.
   C. Buyers who rely on verbal orders feel e-procurement will diminish their influence in the company.
   D. Organizationally, operators fear that e-procurement is leading to the depersonalization of the industry.

   L.O. 2.2

10. Why might a buyer refer to a food Web site maintained by a marketing board rather than a local supplier for information about a particular product?

    A. Food sites contain hyperlinks, while the Web sites of most suppliers do not.
    B. Food sites provide general, industry-wide data rather than information on specific products.
    C. Food sites gather current information from growers, processors, and manufacturers.
    D. Food sites induce buyers to contact them by offering deep discounts and reward programs.

    L.O. 2.1

CHAPTER 3

DISTRIBUTION SYSTEMS

Learning Objectives

After reading this chapter, you should be able to:

3.1   Outline the distribution system in the hospitality industry.

3.2   Explain the economic values added to products and services as they journey through the channel of distribution.

3.3   Evaluate the determination of optimal values and supplier services in the hospitality industry.

Chapter 3 Study Outline

1. The **Efficient Foodservice Response,** or **EFR** initiative, was conceived to analyze opportunities for all industry segments to reduce costs and improve overall supply-chain effectiveness.

2. The three major sources that supply products to hospitality operations are growers, manufacturers, and processors.

    *   **Growers** include farmers and ranchers who provide fresh food products.

    *   **Manufacturers** control the production of an item from raw materials.

    *   **Processors** combine one or more food products and assemble them into a new "value-added" product.

3. **Intermediaries** are the middlemen of the supply chain, helping ensure that products get from sources to retailers.

    *   Intermediaries include: distributors, brokers, manufacturers' representatives, manufacturers' agents, commissaries, wholesale clubs, buying clubs, and e-commerce enablers.

4. Sources for beverage-alcohol products include brewers, wine makers, and distillers, while the major beverage intermediaries are importers/wholesalers, distributors, and alcohol beverage commissions (ABCs).

5. Manufacturers are the major source for furniture, fixtures, and equipment, or FFE items.
   - FFE intermediaries include: dealers, brokers, designers, architects, construction contractors, distributors, and leasing companies.
6. While most sources for services are local, buyers should make sure of a service provider's expertise before hiring them.
7. **Retailers** in the hospitality industry include any operation that sells a product or service directly to consumers.
8. The cost of an item increases as it passes through the distribution channel, with value being added by any or all of the following:
   - **Time value** is generated both when the cost of storing goods until they are bought is taken into account, and when a retailer is allowed to pay for the goods at a later date (buying on credit).
   - **Form value** is added whenever a raw ingredient is transformed into a form that is more user-friendly.
   - **Place value** refers to the additional costs that come from transporting an item from its source to its retail destination.
   - **Information value** refers to recipes, directions, and other pieces of information that one source may provide to make a product easier to use.
   - **Supplier services value** encompasses any number of services that a supplier provides as a convenience to the retailer.
9. In most hospitality operations, buyers deal with several middlemen, but direct buying by large, multiunit corporations and online procurement both have the potential to shorten the supply chain.
   - During poor business conditions, some operations try to cut out middlemen in an effort to provide more of their own economic value. But in doing so, they often ignore the expertise that comes with a middleman's higher price, and they rarely experience increased profitability.
10. Full-time buyers do not usually have total control of the company's economic values, but they do have some responsibility for choosing suppliers based on thorough analysis.
    - Buyers should often consider paying slightly more for a product if it comes with good supplier service, since the extra cost allows the operation to stay focused on its goal of satisfying new and existing customers.

Chapter 3 Exercises

1. Indicate whether each of the following is a source (S) or an intermediary (I) in the distribution system for the product described.

_____a. Restaurant interior designer who incorporates furniture and fixtures into his recommended designs

_____b. Broker who recommends a line of processed food items to operators

_____c. Company that manufactures gin, vodka, and other spirits

_____d. Iowa farmer who grows strawberries, lettuce, and other produce

_____e. Commissary of large quick-service chain

_____f. Processing company that makes frozen pizza dough, frozen prebaked bread, and prebaked pie shells

_____g. Full-line distributor that provides both food and nonfood supplies to operators

_____h. Full-service dealer that carries large foodservice equipment for use in restaurants

_____i. Company that manufactures napkins, paper towels, takeout bags, and paper cups

_____j. Beer brewing company

L.O. 3.1

2. Provide one example of a cost that is tacked on as each of the following items journeys through the distribution channel. Be sure to cover all of the economic values: time, form, place, and information.

   a. Canned corn

   _____

   b. Fresh strawberries

   _____

   c. Refrigerator

   _____

   d. Veal

   _____

L.O. 3.2

3. Sales are down at Cannery Row, a fine-dining seafood restaurant. A sales representative from a new seafood supplier claims he can offer pricing at 12% markup over his cost. His current supplier generally has a 15% markup, but constantly provides excellent service. Knowing that the restaurant currently averages $25,000 a month on seafood, and given that Cannery Row is open everyday from 11–2 P.M. and 5–10 P.M., calculate the additional cost per operating hour that the buyer is paying for his current supplier.

_____

_____

_____

L.O. 3.3

4. Despite the fact that sales are down, offer some reasons why Cannery Row's buyer might want to continue his relationship with his current supplier.

_____

_____

_____

L.O. 3.3

Chapter 3 Check-in

1. EFR was initially conceived to do which of the following?

    A. Increase costs
    B. Improve supply-chain effectiveness
    C. Enhance communication channels
    D. Reduce employee turnover

    L.O. 3.1

2. Which source controls the production of an item from raw materials?

    A. Growers
    B. Manufacturers
    C. Processors
    D. Importers

    L.O. 3.1

3. Which of the following is *not* considered an intermediary?

    A. Distributor
    B. Commissary
    C. Manufacturer
    D. Wholesale club

    L.O. 3.1

4. Which of the following best describes the main difference between a grower and a processor?

   A. Growers provide the raw materials that processors use to make value-added products.
   B. One is a source; the other is an intermediary.
   C. A processor typically adds less value than a grower does.
   D. Processors sell only to a retailer, whereas growers sell to everyone.

L.O. 3.1

5. The additional price a buyer pays for having a product stored off-site until it is needed is known as

   A. place value.
   B. information value.
   C. form value.
   D. time value.

L.O. 3.2

6. A produce supplier who precuts broccoli into bite-sized chunks is adding which type of value?

   A. Time value
   B. Service supplier value
   C. Form value
   D. Information value

L.O. 3.2

7. Someone who sells a product or service to its ultimate consumer is called a

   A. broad-line distributor.
   B. retailer.
   C. fabricator.
   D. merchant wholesaler.

L.O. 3.1

8. The form value is very expensive because highly processed items are usually

   A. of corresponding high quality.
   B. in high demand.
   C. packaged in costly containers.
   D. considered an investment.

L.O. 3.2

9. Most companies that have eliminated the middleman have

   A. not been able to increase their profitability.
   B. experienced high inventory turnover.
   C. been forced to increase work-week hours.
   D. purchasing experts on staff.

L.O. 3.3

10. When managers consider the feasibility of providing their own economic values, they usually

   A. decide it is too costly.
   B. employ consultants to help them make decisions.
   C. slant the analyses in the direction they desire.
   D. ignore potential antitrust problems.

L.O. 3.3

CHAPTER 4

FORCES AFFECTING THE DISTRIBUTION SYSTEMS

Learning Objectives

After reading this chapter, you should be able to:

4.1   Identify the economic forces that affect the channel of distribution.

4.2   Identify the political issues that affect the channel of distribution.

4.3   Identify the legal restrictions that affect the channel of distribution.

4.4   Identify the technological advances that affect the channel of distribution.

Chapter 4 Study Outline

1. **Supply** and **demand** considerations have a powerful effect on purchase prices.

    - When demand for a product exceeds its supply, its price will rise; when supply of a product exceeds demand for it, its price will fall.

2. The **value** of a product is directly related to its **quality** (as perceived by the buyer) plus the **supplier services** that accompany it (again, based on the relative worth of these services to the buyer), but inversely related to its **edible-portion**, or **EP**, cost (the final cost of a product by the time it appears on the customer's table).

3. Sellers in the hospitality industry often try to create a state of **monopolistic competition** with their products.

    - In monopolistic competition, the seller enjoys a monopoly based on the buyer's perception that the seller's product is unique and cannot be readily substituted, resulting in a price that is controlled more by the seller and less by supply and demand forces.

    - All members of the distribution channel highlight value over price in an attempt to retain price control over their products (i.e., create a state of monopolistic competition).

4. Since laws and regulations strongly influence how hospitality operators conduct business, members of the foodservice industry are actively involved in political lobbying efforts on the local, state, and federal levels.

    - In general, primary sources have the most political influence, as there are fewer of them compared to other intermediaries, and they have a more focused set of interests.

16

- Political activity refers not only to legislation, but also includes a series of "unwritten laws" that govern behavior between different members of the distribution channel.

5. Ethical and unethical forces in the distribution channel continue to influence product availability and prices.

- Pressure on both salespersons and buyers to make attractive deals all too often provides an incentive toward unethical practices, such as the offering and acceptance of gifts.

- In the long run, an honest manager will advance more quickly than a dishonest manager who constantly has to cover his/her tracks.

- Several purchasing associations have developed codes of ethics to guide their members in ethical behavior, and both buyers and their managers should be familiar with these guidelines.

6. In the past century, many federal laws have controlled the flow of food from suppliers to foodservice operators to consumers.

- Passed in 1890, the **Sherman Act** restricts any action by a company that tends to eliminate or severely reduce competition.

- Upton Sinclair's shocking accounts of the meatpacking industry in his novel, *The Jungle,* led to passage of the **Pure Food Act** (1906) and the **Meat Inspection Act** (1907). Both acts gave the USDA inspection powers throughout the channels of distribution; the agency continues to use this authority to assure the safety of the nation's red meat, poultry, and eggs.

- The **Federal Food, Drug, and Cosmetic Act** (1906) established the Food and Drug Administration (FDA) to inspect products, records, and premises of food and drug establishments to ensure compliance with the law.

- While there is no rigorous, mandatory inspection program for seafood, many fish processors participate in voluntary continuous inspection programs. In 1997, the FDA established Hazard Analysis Critical Control Point (HACCP) requirements for all processors.

- Like the Sherman Act, the **Clayton Act** (1914) increased the federal government's control over antitrust violations by making it illegal for sellers to engage in either **tying agreements** (deals in which a seller forces a buyer to purchase one product in order to receive another product) or **exclusive dealing** (deals in which a seller forces a buyer to buy only his/her product).

- The **Robinson-Patman Act** (1936) created more antitrust legislation that made it illegal to give **promotional discounts** to some qualified buyers but not others. It also established a **quantity limits provision** that set at a reasonable level the number of items a buyer must purchase before receiving discount pricing. Finally, it outlawed **predatory pricing,** a practice in which sellers try to drive competitors out of a market by selling their products at a price below their cost, so the seller can create more of a monopoly in that market.

- The **Hart Act** (1966–1969) sought to eliminate misleading descriptions and illustrations on packaging, and its passage prompted many primary sources to voluntarily adopt a series of labeling regulations that are still used today.

7. Buyers and sellers must also consider contract principles, the authority operators delegate to their buyers, the precise moment the title to any product passes, warranties and guarantees, patent procedures, and rebates.

    - In general, purchase orders over five hundred dollars need to be written for them to stand as enforceable contracts.

    - In direct-buying agreements, the buyer takes **title** of goods (i.e., owns them) once the merchandise leaves the primary source's premises. The goods travel to the buyer by common carrier marked as **"free on board"** or **FOB**, a legal term that clearly defines the goods as the responsibility of the buyer.

8. Technological advances affecting the purchasing process include genetic engineering of food, improved preservation methods, faster transportation, computerized operations, and efficient packaging.

Chapter 4 Exercises

All of the following statements are false. Rewrite each statement so that it is correct.

1. The equalizing forces of supply and demand are so powerful that they set prices for all commodities.

_____

_____

L.O. 4.1

2. A product's perceived EP (edible portion) cost is usually equal to its AP (as purchased) cost.

_____

_____

L.O. 4.1

3. Perceived value tends to be uniform from person to person.

_____

_____

L.O. 4.1

4. Ethical behavior in purchasing is clear-cut and easily defined among operators and distributors.

_____

_____

L.O. 4.2

5. Meat is among the least regulated types of food in the U.S.

_____

_____

L.O. 4.3

6. Numerous government officials must scrutinize a packaged piece of fish before it can be sold.

_____

_____

L.O. 4.3

7. A tying agreement is a legal agreement in which a manufacturer chooses a few selected distributors to sell its products.

_____

_____

_____

L.O. 4.3

8. Companies are forced by law to list all ingredients in descending order, from greatest proportion to least proportion, for all packaged, processed food.

_____

_____

_____

L.O. 4.3

9. A verbal purchasing order of four hundred dollars would never be an enforceable contract according to the law.

_____

_____

_____

L.O. 4.3

10. When purchasing from intermediaries, a hospitality operation usually takes title at the moment the merchandise leaves the primary source's premises.

_____

_____

_____

L.O. 4.3

11. The principle reason that hospitality operators usually buy value-added items, such as convenience food items, is to enhance quality.

_____

_____

_____

L.O. 4.4

12. The primary advantage of Controlled Atmosphere Packaging (CAP) to the buyer/operator is its low cost.

_____

_____

L.O. 4.4

13. Buyers must react to intangible forces, as well as economic, political, ethical, legal, and technological ones.

_____

_____

L.O. 4.4

20

Chapter 4 Check-in

1. If the demand for a product exceeds supply, the price for that product will
    A. increase.
    B. decrease.
    C. stay the same.
    L.O. 4.1

2. The perceived quality of a product plus the perceived supplier services divided by the perceived edible-portion cost equals the product's
    A. as-served cost.
    B. perceived value.
    C. as-used cost.
    D. final value.
    L.O. 4.1

3. Which members in the channel of distribution have the most political influence?
    A. Intermediaries
    B. Lobbyists
    C. Primary sources
    D. Contractors
    L.O. 4.2

4. Which of the following is true about the ethical force on prices and availability of the products that hospitality operations need?
    A. Most managers consider accepting gifts from suppliers unethical.
    B. A dishonest manager can advance more surely than an honest one.
    C. There is no clear-cut definition of ethical behavior.
    D. Ethical and unethical forces do not influence product prices and availability significantly.
    L.O. 4.2

5. Upton Sinclair's description of horrendous sanitation conditions in the meat-packing industry during the early 1900s led to the passage of the
    A. Sherman Act.
    B. Federal Food, Drug, and Cosmetic Act.
    C. Pathogen Reduction and Hazard Analysis Critical Control Points system assessment.
    D. Pure Food Act and the Meat Inspection Act.
    L.O. 4.3

6. Which of the following is not subject to mandatory continuous inspection?
    A. Beef
    B. Poultry
    C. Seafood
    D. Veal
    L.O. 4.3

7. Which of the following can sellers do under the Clayton Act and the Robinson–Patman Act?
    A. Give promotional discounts to buyers of their choice.
    B. Determine minimum-quantity purchase requirements for buyers to qualify for discounts.
    C. Price products exceptionally low to eliminate competitors from the marketplace.
    D. Accept payment of two different prices for the same product if one buyer provides some value.
    L.O. 4.3

8. A purchase order of five hundred dollars or more is not enforceable in a court of law unless the agreement is

A. in writing.
B. notarized.
C. approved by management.
D. accepted on consignment.

L.O. 4.3

9. Once a product has been placed on a common carrier "free on board," who owns the product and takes responsibility for its safe transit?

A. Primary source
B. Buyer
C. Common carrier
D. Insurance company

L.O. 4.3

10. In general, processed food products have

A. higher packaging costs.
B. lower packaging costs.
C. similar packaging costs.
D. unrelated packaging costs.

L.O. 4.4

CHAPTER 5

AN OVERVIEW OF THE PURCHASING FUNCTION

Learning Objectives

After reading this chapter, you should be able to:

5.1   Describe the purchasing activities in a hospitality operation.

5.2   Determine the purchasing requirements of a hospitality operation using value

analysis, what-if analysis, and make-or-buy analysis.

5.3   Outline the objectives of the purchasing function and the potential problems that

buyers encounter when pursuing those objectives.

Chapter 5 Study Outline

1. Purchasing agents or buyers in a hospitality operation generally perform
    the following activities:

- Develop a selection and procurement plan.

- Determine product requirements.

- Select from existing suppliers or source new ones.

- Maintain sufficient inventory levels.

- Negotiate AP prices, delivery schedules, and other supplier services with suppliers.

- Conduct ongoing research, including various types of value analysis.

- Visit suppliers' facilities to ensure they are quality operations.

- Maintain good relationships with all current and potential suppliers.

- Educate suppliers about current and future needs.

- Purchase, receive, store, and issue all incoming products.

- Dispose of excess and unsalable items.

- Recycle items whenever possible.

- Develop record-keeping controls.

- Organize and administer the purchasing function (in large operations).

- Continuously improve your buying performance.

- Maintain good relationships with competitors (e.g., lend them stock if they run out—one day they will return the favor).

2. Value analysis is the formal process of exploring ways to increase the value of a product or service by increasing either its quality or supplier services, or by reducing its EP cost.

   - Buyers should always consult with the people who actually use a product or service, as they may have good reasons for wanting a product with a slightly higher EP cost.

   - Using computer spreadsheet software and mathematical models, buyers explore **what-if analysis**, such as *Increase in overall food cost = % price increase for an ingredient × Ingredient's % of overall food cost.*

   - **Make-or-Buy Analysis** involves a buyer evaluating whether or not an operation should prepare an item in-house or buy a premade or value-added product.

3. The five primary objectives of the purchasing function are:

   - Maintain adequate supply of product and services.

   - Minimize investments yet avoid stockouts between deliveries.

   - Maintain product quality by requiring consistency of products and services over time.

   - Understand the difference between AP and EP costs, and strive to obtain the lowest possible EP cost.

   - Maintain a competitive position by getting a good deal from suppliers in terms of both cost and services.

4. Problems that buyers frequently encounter include:

   - **Backdoor selling**, in which a salesperson makes a sales pitch to another employee, who then pressures the buyer to buy the product or service

   - Excessive time spent with salespeople, unless times that salespeople may call are clearly stated

   - Ethical traps that accompany the acceptance of gifts or special favors

   - Lack of authority to fully carry out the job

   - Lack of time to do the job right

   - Difficulty working with other department heads

   - Late deliveries, "back orders," and unacceptable substitutions by suppliers

   - Lack of appreciation by other personnel of the buyer's direct role in creating profit

   - Lack of service by suppliers (especially true in smaller operations)

   - Receiving and storage inadequacies that result in excessive spoilage, waste, or theft

   - Excessive time/effort spent on returns and allowances of unsuitable merchandise

5. Technological enhancements are helping buyers do their jobs more quickly, which allows them more time to do their jobs more effectively.

Chapter 5 Exercises

1. Put the following purchasing activities in sequential order. Use the numbers 1 (for the first activity) to 7 (for the last) for each activity in the purchasing process.

_____a. Select suppliers.

_____b. Negotiate specific AP prices, delivery schedules, and other services.

_____c. Establish the varieties and amounts of products and services required.

_____d. Receive, store, and issue products.

_____e. Conduct the sourcing process.

_____f. Determine policies and procedures to guide the purchasing function.

_____g. Purchase products.

L.O. 5.1

2. Indicate what kind of analysis is being described below.

   a. A buyer examines a product to determine whether it makes more sense to buy the product premade or to make it from scratch.

   _____

   b. A buyer examines a product to determine if there are any unnecessary costs that can be eliminated.

   _____

   c. A buyer examines how overall food and labor costs will be affected by a change in purchasing.

   _____

L.O. 5.2

3. What problems might befall a buyer whose only concern is to minimize the amount of stock on hand in a foodservice operation?

   _____

   _____

   _____

L.O. 5.3

4. Explain why the owner of a hot dog stand might justify paying a higher AP price for a leaner grade of hot dogs.

_____

_____

_____

L.O. 5.3

5. Charlotte does the buying for Deli Delites, a small deli in the suburbs of Detroit. Before she can actually place an order, she must get approval from Sandra, the owner of the operation. Many of the suppliers have become friendly with Sandra and often go directly to her when they make deliveries. In addition to buying, Charlotte is responsible for receiving, storing, issuing, and accounting. Identify three possible problems that Charlotte might face as a buyer for Deli Delites.

- _____

- _____

- _____

L.O. 5.3

Chapter 5 Check-in

1. A selection and procurement plan should contain which of the following?

   A. Discussion of purchasing trends
   B. Quantities of product required
   C. Overview of local competition
   D. Organization chart

   L.O. 5.1

2. The process of a buyer creating a supplier who can fulfill a unique product need is usually referred to as

   A. sourcing.
   B. selection.
   C. forecasting.
   D. negotiation.

   L.O. 5.1

3. To achieve optimal inventory management, an operator must do which of the following?

   A. Negotiate specific AP prices.
   B. Visit suppliers' facilities.
   C. Ensure that an appropriate inventory of all items is always on hand.
   D. Avoid ethical traps.

   L.O. 5.1

4. Claude usually buys real whipping cream for the bakery items at Chez Claude. He is currently interested in researching the possibility of using a less expensive substitute if the bakery items can be prepared without a discernable loss of quality. What kind of analysis is Claude doing?

A. Value analysis
B. Forecasting
C. What-if analysis
D. Make-or-buy analysis

L.O. 5.2

5. If the price of pork tenderloin is expected to increase 15% and pork tenderloin represents 20% of an operation's overall food cost, what will be the overall effect on the operation's food cost?

A. 0.03% increase
B. 0.3% increase
C. 3% increase
D. 30% increase

L.O. 5.2

6. The analysis in the previous question is often referred to as

A. forecasting analysis.
B. what-if analysis.
C. value analysis.
D. make-or-buy analysis.

L.O. 5.2

7. The major disadvantage of convenience food items is

A. reduced employee skill requirements.
B. high price.
C. increase in ordering costs.
D. less foodhandler supervision.

L.O. 5.2

8. Operators must strive to find some kind of trade-off between investing in inventory and

A. maintaining quality.
B. obtaining the lowest possible EP cost.
C. maintaining the operation's competitive position.
D. running out of product.

L.O. 5.3

9. When a salesperson bypasses the buyer and goes to some other employee to make a sales pitch, this practice is called

A. backdoor selling.
B. trapping.
C. playing the field.
D. sabotage.

L.O. 5.3

10. When a supplier does not have something that a buyer has ordered, he or she may note that the item is

A. undesirable.
B. discounted.
C. substituted.
D. back-ordered.

L.O. 5.3

CHAPTER 6

THE ORGANIZATION AND ADMINISTRATION OF PURCHASING

Learning Objectives

After reading this chapter, you should be able to:

6.1   Describe the methods used to plan and organize the purchasing activities of a

hospitality operator.

6.2   Recognize the issues involved in administering the purchasing activities of a

hospitality operator.

Chapter 6 Study Outline

1. An effective **purchasing plan** seeks to strike a balance among the five purchasing objectives.
   - Decisions made at the initial stages of a purchasing plan need to take into account the overall goals and objectives of the operation.
2. The process of organizing the purchasing function involves putting human and material resources in place to support the goals of the purchasing plan.
3. In general, there are two basic organizational patterns for purchasing: one for the independent operators and one for multiunit chain operations.
4. While numerous variations occur, the organizational pattern for independent operations all share one common characteristic: the owner-manager tends to be directly involved in purchasing.
   - The larger the independent operation, the more portions of the purchasing function are divided up among department heads and/or purchasing specialists.
   - While medium-sized operations rarely employ full-time buyers, crucial employees such as the chef, the head bartender, and the dining room supervisor are often designated as "user-buyers." They become responsible for a portion of the purchasing function.
5. Chains have an additional level of management whose responsibilities specifically revolve around the purchasing function.
   - The level of purchasing independence at the unit level varies, depending on whether the unit's manager is a franchisee or a person hired to run a company-owned store.

Franchisees, in general, have more independence, although their choices are usually controlled by standards and vendors dictated by the corporate vice president of purchasing.

- Responsibilities of the vice president of purchasing include: setting purchasing guidelines for unit managers; negotiating national, long-term contracts; setting purchase specifications; performing research activities; serving as a resource for unit managers; and often supervising a chain's commissary.
- While centralized purchasing reduces AP prices through quantity buys, it has the potential to alienate local suppliers.

6. The job specifications for full- or part-time buyers typically are divided into three broad areas of **technical, conceptual,** and **human skills.**

- Training for entry-level purchasing personnel should include an orientation to the job and the company, formal instruction, and on-the-job experience.

7. For full- and part-time buyers, budgeting the needs of their purchasing department, managing their personnel, and controlling waste, spoilage, and theft are often crucial tasks of the position.

- In larger operations, products are often controlled through an "indirect control system," in which a system of computerized or written forms enables the controller to monitor all products.

Chapter 6 Exercises

1. Indicate whether each of the following is true (T) or false (F). If false, rewrite the statement so that it is correct.

_____(a) Devising one specific way of working toward the hospitality operation's goals is the major accomplishment of the planning stage.

_____

_____

_____(b) Planning for purchasing is part of the overall plan of the hospitality organization and cannot exist apart from the overall goals of the operation.

_____

_____

_____(c) In large hospitality operations, the head bartender, the chef, the dining room supervisor, and other supervisors tend to do some buying as part of their other responsibilities.

_____

_____

_____(d) Purchasing in independent operations always involves the owner/manager, regardless of the operation's size.

_____

_____

_____(e) Compared to managers hired to run a company-owned unit, a franchisee unit manager usually has only a small degree of independence in the purchasing function.

_____

_____

_____(f) There is little evidence to suggest that the commissary and central distribution network is a cost-effective system.

_____

_____

_____(g) The most important training an entry-level purchasing employee can receive is on-the-job training.

_____

_____

_____(h) Supervisory style is a personal choice.

_____

_____

L.O. 6.1, 6.2

2. What determines whether or not a foodservice operation will employ a full-time buyer?

_____

_____

_____

L.O. 6.1

3. What type of foodservice operation is most likely to participate in a co-op buying group?

_____

L.O. 6.1

4. List three responsibilities or tasks commonly performed by a vice president of purchasing of a chain company.

- _____

- _____

- _____

L.O. 6.2

5. Why is product control such an important part of the purchasing function?

_____

_____

_____

L.O. 6.2

Chapter 6 Check-in

1. Decisions made at the initial planning stage
   A. are based on intuition.
   B. set the tone for future activities.
   C. change continuously throughout the purchasing process.
   D. are the sole responsibility of the buyer.
   L.O. 6.1

2. Generally, how many major organizational patterns for buying activity are found in the hospitality industry?
   A. One
   B. Two
   C. Three
   D. Four
   L.O. 6.1

3. In small hospitality operations, selection and procurement are whose responsibility?
   A. Owner/manager
   B. Buyer
   C. Accountant
   D. Secretary
   L.O. 6.1

4. Medium-sized operations tend to designate one or two employees as
   A. user-buyers.
   B. part-time buyers.
   C. full-time buyers.
   D. special buyers.
   L.O. 6.1

5. Communal-buying networks operate particularly well when independents agree to

   A. buy only generic product.
   B. use the same brands.
   C. place small orders.
   D. be directly involved in purchasing.

   L.O. 6.1

6. Managers of company-owned stores have the same options as franchisees, but

   A. fewer benefits.
   B. lower salaries.
   C. less flexibility.
   D. more employees.

   L.O. 6.1

7. The job specification for purchasing employees includes which three areas of skills?

   A. Reading, computation, people
   B. Abstract, concrete, developmental
   C. Technical, conceptual, human
   D. Word processing, mathematical, manual

   L.O. 6.2

8. Entry-level purchasing personnel typically require what kind of training?

   A. Management training seminars
   B. Word processing
   C. Formal instruction
   D. Certification

   L.O. 6.2

9. Operations that employ user-buyers rarely

   A. enjoy healthy profits.
   B. negotiate prices with suppliers.
   C. create a separate purchasing budget.
   D. dictate any type of supervisory policy.

   L.O. 6.2

10. A system of overlapping computerized and/or noncomputerized forms that allow an employee to keep tabs on all products is called a(n)

   A. commissary.
   B. national contract system.
   C. direct control system.
   D. indirect control system.

   L.O. 6.2

CHAPTER 7

THE BUYER'S RELATIONS WITH OTHER COMPANY PERSONNEL

Learning Objectives

After reading this chapter, you should be able to:

7.1   Describe the buyer's relationship to others in the hospitality organization.

7.2   Give examples of selection and procurement policies a buyer may be required to follow.

7.3   Explain various methods used to evaluate a buyer's performance.

Chapter 7 Study Outline

1. Most buyers or buyer-managers answer to a supervisor in the organization.

    *   The job specification for a buyer lists the technical, interpersonal, and conceptual skills necessary for good performance.

    *   A buyer's job description lists the actual duties that the buyer must perform, from carrying out the general objectives of the purchasing function to selection and procurement policies.

2. **Selection and procurement policies** guide a buyer in how to act and what to do in various situations.

    *   A buyer who accept gifts from a supplier risks an obligation to do business with that supplier, regardless of how well the supplier's products and prices fit into the buyer's purchasing plan.

    *   Supervisors often insist that an approved supplier list be developed to avoid backdoor selling situations.

    *   Supervisors often restrict the amount of goods and services buyers can purchase from any one supplier without additional permission.

    *   Key products often have flexible price limits placed on them, so that an increase of its price above the limit triggers value analysis by the buyer.

    *   While some operations allow employees to purchase items for their personal use, supervisors generally discourage this practice.

    *   Buyers should avoid **reciprocal arrangements** ("you buy from me if I buy from you"), as they are illegal and rarely benefit the buyer.

- Sample products or equipment should be accepted only if there is a serious interest in the item.
- Buyers who purchase a large quantity or volume from a supplier often receive a discount; other discounts are typically awarded for prompt payments (e.g., cash discount) and as an incentive to promote a product with an operation's customers (e.g., promotional discount).
- Most hospitality operations have a written set of ethical guidelines that buyers are required to follow.
- Buyers in small operations often are responsible for product until it is issued into production.
- Other guidelines a buyer may be required to follow include supporting local suppliers; following quality standards created by a supervisor; and using shopping procedures to ensure that several suppliers are considered for each product category.

3. Full-time and part-time buyers usually receive a straight salary; part-time buyers tend to earn salaries based on several duties, not just buying.

4. Buyers are evaluated on two types of performance criteria: **operational performance** and **procurement performance**.
   - Operational performance relates to how well a buyer adheres to the purchasing department's allocated budget.
   - Though the procurement performance is difficult to gauge, supervisors tend to consider one or many of the following indicators: materials budget; inventory turnover; percentage of sales volume; stockouts; number of late deliveries, returned items, or back orders; and periodic checks of other suppliers' AP prices for large discrepancies with current supplier's prices (a clue that the buyer might be negligent or even dishonest).
   - In general, supervisors should establish clearly defined and easily measured goals to determine a buyer's performance.

5. While a buyer's job competence and good performance are essential, supervisors generally also expect buyers to behave in a way that always considers the best interests of the operation.

6. Buyers expect supervisors to give them the necessary authority to do their jobs adequately; to give them the necessary budget and facilities to carry out their job; to let them have a voice in major buying decisions; and to appreciate the profit potential of the buying activity.

7. Cooperation and coordination are essential to the relationships between buyers and their colleagues.
   - Buyers and production supervisors often have conflicts over whether high waste and spoilage is due to inferior merchandise purchases or to wasteful food preparation.

- While the use of buyer-user positions can often avoid these types of conflicts, such a solution has the drawback of eliminating a crucial check and balance that can uncover buying mistakes.

7. The buyer's primary responsibility to hourly employees is to provide the resources they need to perform their jobs.
   - Conflicts tend to occur between buyers and hourly employees when buyers overstep their control and authority. To avoid these situations, buyers should work with the hourly employees' supervisor(s) to ensure that hourly employees minimize waste and spoilage.

Chapter 7 Exercises

1. Carla is the general manager of all food services for a community college. She has performed all purchasing functions herself for the past four years, but a recent increase in student enrollment has allowed her to hire a new purchaser. She is now writing a job description, including job specifications, for the position.

   (1) Circle the appropriate technical skill to include in the job-specification portion of the job description.
      a. Ability to negotiate with suppliers
      b. Ability to lift loads of at least twenty-five pounds
      c. Ability to plan and organize for future purchasing needs
      d. Ability to write purchase specifications for food, beverage, and nonfood supplies

   (2) Circle the appropriate interpersonal skill to include in the job-specification portion of the job description.
      a. Ability to negotiate with suppliers
      b. Ability to lift loads of at least twenty-five pounds
      c. Ability to plan and organize for future purchasing needs
      d. Ability to write purchase specifications for food, beverage, and nonfood supplies

   (3) Circle the appropriate conceptual skill to include in the job-specification portion of the job description.
      a. Ability to negotiate with suppliers
      b. Ability to lift loads of at least twenty-five pounds
      c. Ability to plan and organize for future purchasing needs
      d. Ability to write purchase specifications for food, beverage, and nonfood supplies

L.O. 7.3

2. Vladis is the food and beverage operations director for a large hotel. Operations have become complex and extensive enough that he has decided to hire a full-time purchasing director.

(1) Write a job description for the position, including the responsibilities and tasks of the position and the person to whom the purchasing director will report.

_____

_____

_____

_____

_____

_____

_____

(2) Write a job specification for the purchasing director, including the qualities and technical, interpersonal, and conceptual skills you are seeking in the person filling the position.

_____

_____

_____

_____

_____

_____

_____

L.O. 7.1, 7.3

3. Name three situations that might be addressed by a hospitality operation's selection and procurement policies.

- _____

- _____

- _____

L.O. 7.2

4. Use a check mark to indicate which of the following can help a supervisor evaluate a buyer's procurement performance.

_____Materials budget

_____Number of stockouts

_____Loyalty to the company

_____Inventory turnover

_____Ability to be fair and impartial

_____Ethics

_____Percentage of sales volume

_____Interpersonal skills

L.O. 7.3

5. Name three expectations that

   a. supervisors have of buyers.

-    _____

-    _____

-    _____

   b. buyers have of their supervisors.

-    _____

-    _____

-    _____

L.O. 7.1

Chapter 7 Check-in

1. Conducting a performance appraisal is an example of which of the following skills?

   A. Technical
   B. Conceptual
   C. Interpersonal
   D. Ethical

   L.O. 7.1

2. When recruiting a part-time buyer, the main question to consider is

   A. where to find potential applicants.
   B. the appropriate salary range to be paid.
   C. the emphasis attached to the individual aspects of the job.
   D. the hours to be worked.

   L.O. 7.1

3. Which of the following might be covered by an operation's selection and procurement policies?

   A. Accepting gifts from a supplier
   B. Storing excess inventory
   C. Minimizing errors
   D. Purchasing at the right price

   L.O. 7.2

4. What type of discount is often offered to a buyer who purchases a large amount of one specific type of merchandise?

   A. Volume discount
   B. Cash discount
   C. Promotional discount
   D. Quantity discount

   L.O. 7.2

5. In small operations, the user-buyer usually takes responsibility for an item until it is

   A. received.
   B. used in production.
   C. stored.
   D. paid in full.

   L.O. 7.2

6. How well a buyer has adhered to the purchasing department's allocated budget is called

   A. operational performance.
   B. procurement performance.
   C. material performance.
   D. percentage performance.

   L.O. 7.3

7. Which of the following indicators is *not* generally used to evaluate procurement performance?

   A. Inventory turnover
   B. Periodic check of AP prices among other suppliers
   C. Number of late deliveries
   D. Number of meals served

   L.O. 7.3

8. If a restaurant's annual cost of goods sold is $140,000, beginning inventory is $7,000, and ending inventory is $4,500, what is the operation's inventory turnover?

   A. 21
   B. 22
   C. 23
   D. 24

   L.O. 7.2

9. To avoid backdoor selling situations, supervisors often insist on the development of _____ as part of an operation's selection and procurement policies.

    A. Supplier lists
    B. Accurate receiving procedures
    C. Inventory-turnover rates
    D. Regular employee meetings

L.O. 7.2

10. What is the major potential conflict that can occur between buyers and hourly employees?

    A. Number of returned products, late deliveries, and back orders may exceed acceptable levels.
    B. Hourly employees may not be loyal to the company.
    C. Hourly employees may not have the necessary authority to perform their jobs adequately.
    D. Buyer may try to exert authority over employees supervised by someone else.

L.O. 7.1

CHAPTER 8

THE PURCHASE SPECIFICATION: AN OVERALL VIEW

Learning Objectives

After reading this chapter, you should be able to:

8.1   Explain the purpose of the purchase specification.

8.2   List the information included on the purchase specification.

8.3   Identify factors that influence the information included on the purchase specification.

8.4   Explain the potential problems related to purchase specifications.

8.5   Describe how quality is measured, including the use of government grades and packers' brands.

Chapter 8 Study Outline

1. Top management typically sets standards for both **product specifications** and **purchase specifications**, and buyers or users then handle the details.

2. There are five main reasons to create purchase specifications:

    *   They create quality-control and cost-control standards.
    *   They help avoid misunderstandings between suppliers, buyers, users, and other company officials.
    *   They provide back-up information for times when a buyer is unavailable.
    *   They can serve as useful training tools for trainees.
    *   They include all relevant details necessary for multiple suppliers to provide comparable bids.

3. Purchase specifications generally include several of the following:

    *   Performance requirement—the intended use of the product or service
    *   Exact name of the product or service
    *   Packer's brand name, if appropriate, along with the phrase "or equivalent"—so suppliers who carry other brands can offer bids
    *   U.S. quality grade, if appropriate, with "or equivalent"—so suppliers who have not graded can offer bids

- Size information, either by weight, or by "count" (number of items per pound or per ten pounds)
- Acceptable trim, or the maximum amount of waste tolerated for an item—an especially important spec
- for fresh meat or produce
- Package size
- Type of package, including any requirements regarding recyclable packaging materials
- Preservation and/or processing method—refrigerated, frozen, canned, or numerous other distinctions
- Point of origin: an especially important consideration with fish
- Packaging procedure
- Degree of ripeness: important for fresh produce and aged meats or wine
- Form: important with processed items such as cheese
- Color
- Trade association standards
- Approved substitutes—to minimize stockouts and reduce calls to buyers when a product shortage occurs
- Expiration date
- Chemical standards, such as requirements that produce be certified organic
- Test or inspection procedures to be used to ensure delivered items perform adequately
- Cost and quantity limitations
- General instructions relating to delivery, credit terms, allowable number of returns and stockouts, product availability for all units in a multiunit operation, and other supplier services
- Specific instructions related to bidding

4. Factors that influence which information should be included in a purchase specification include:
- Company goals and policies
- Available time and money
- Production systems used by the hospitality operation
- Storage facilities
- Employee skill levels
- Menu requirements
- Sales prices or budgetary limitations

- Service style of the operation (e.g., cafeterias often need products with long hot-holding life)

5. Specs are typically written by company personnel, adapted from industry and government publications, created by a hired expert, or written in cooperation with both buyer and seller.

6. While writing specs creates many benefits, it can also pose some costs to an operation, including some cleverly hidden problems. Problems with specs can include:

   - Higher AP prices due to unreasonable delivery requirements or other limits based on quality tolerance, cost, or quantity

   - Lack of supplier eligibility due to overly precise or tight specs

   - Levels of quality set too high, resulting in specs no supplier can provide

   - Overreliance on government grades

   - Lack of periodic revisions to the specs

   - Lack of expertise among receiving personnel

   - Getting hit with an initial "**lowball**" bid by a supplier as a means of getting an operation's business, only to pay more over time as the supplier trades the buyer up to more expensive products and services

   - Loose specs that allow less-reliable suppliers into the bidding process

   - **Redundant favoritism**, in which a buyer routinely chooses one supplier over others no matter how competitive their bids are. Such practices waste other suppliers' time, and may make it difficult to work with them should the primary supplier fall out of favor.

   - Scheduling several deliveries at the same time

7. Quality is a standard that hospitality operators develop or decide upon, then strive to maintain in their operation.

   - To arrive at a quality standard, many operations conduct market research to assess their customers' expectations of quality.

8. Several objective measurements of quality are available, including **federal government grades**, AP prices, and **packers' brands**.

   - The USDA grades more than three hundred food products, usually through a scorecard approach that requires a product to score eighty-five to ninety points or more in order to attain the highest grade designation.

   - To be graded, a product needs to be under continuous federal-government inspection.

   - Problems with federal-government grades include: an overreliance on appearance rather than taste; a wide tolerance between grades; too much grader discretion; the irrelevance of grades to EP costs; lack of consideration to packaging and delivery's roles in product quality; lack of uniform terminology; and lack of regional designations (i.e., California versus Florida oranges).

- While not a direct relationship, AP prices and quality usually go hand in hand.
- Packers' brands are essentially a food processor's personal grading system that is used in lieu of a federal quality brand.
- Most packers' brands have at least three quality levels that are designated either by a particular nomenclature or by different-colored package labels.
- Buyers also rely on samples, endorsements, and trade associations' quality standards in arriving at their own specifications.

9. The more supplier services written into a spec, the fewer the numbers of suppliers who will be able to provide an operation with exactly what it wants.

Chapter 8 Exercises

1. Who decides what to include on purchase specifications?

_____

_____

L.O. 8. 1

2. Design a general specification form on a separate piece of paper for ordering any type of food product. Include spaces for all of the types of information to be included on the spec.

L.O. 8.2

3. Name at least three factors that influence the types of information included on the specification.

- _____

- _____

- _____

L.O. 8.3

4. Identify which problem related to purchase specifications might result when each of the following occurs.

a. Specifications are too tight.

_____

b. Buyer writes several specs, sends them out for bid, and then rejects all bids except the one from the supplier that the buyer usually buys from anyway.

_____

c. Buyer's specs are too loose.

_____

d. Bids are entered on a three-month contract basis.

_____

e. Suppliers want to woo buyers away from their regular suppliers.

_____

L.O. 8.4

5. How does each of the following help buyers ensure product quality?

a. U.S. government grades

_____

_____

_____

b. Use of packers' brands

_____

_____

_____

L.O. 8.5

Chapter 8 Check-in

1. A description of all of the product characteristics required to fill certain production and/or service needs is called a

A. product specification.
B. purchase specification.
C. price specification.
D. cost specification.

L.O. 8.1

2. Which piece of information is usually considered the most important on a spec?

A. Packer's brand name
B. Performance requirement
C. U.S. quality grade
D. Size information

L.O. 8.1

3. The value of which of the following sometimes exceeds the value of the item to be purchased?

   A. Preservation
   B. Shipping
   C. Packaging
   D. Chemical processing

   L.O. 8.2

4. Which consideration is usually the most important in determining the information to be included on a spec?

   A. Menu requirements
   B. Service style
   C. Time and money available
   D. Company goals and policies

   L.O. 8.3

5. Who tends to write the specs in most independent operations?

   A. Company personnel
   B. Government employees
   C. Hired experts
   D. Buyer and seller, working together

   L.O. 8.3

6. Specifications that request a quality difficult for suppliers to provide can often add to a product's _____.

   A. value.
   B. customer satisfaction.
   C. cost.
   D. inequality among bidders.

   L.O. 8.4

7. Writing specifications that are too tight tends to _____.

   A. allow a buyer to concentrate on EP prices.
   B. waste a lot of time, money, and effort.
   C. result in too many eligible suppliers.
   D. alienate a majority of suppliers.

   L.O. 8.4

8. In order to decide on quality standards, hospitality operators must measure the types of quality standards that their

   A. customers expect.
   B. employees expect.
   C. competitors expect.
   D. top management expects.

   L.O. 8.5

9. Which of the following are always produced under continuous federal-government inspection?

   A. Vegetables
   B. Meat items
   C. Rice
   D. Shellfish

   L.O. 8.5

10. A major problem with government grading is the emphasis graders place on _____.

   A. cost.
   B. texture.
   C. appearance.
   D. politics.

   L.O. 8.5

CHAPTER 9

THE OPTIMAL AMOUNT

Learning Objectives

After reading this chapter, you should be able to:

9.1   Calculate the correct order quantities and timing using the par stock, Levinson, and theoretical methods.

9.2   Explain the benefits and problems of using the theoretical method.

Chapter 9 Study Outline

1. A principal objective of inventory management is to maintain only the necessary amounts of food, beverage, and nonfood supplies to serve guests without running out of anything, but not to have so much inventory that the operation suffers from spoilage and other storage costs.

2. The **par stock approach** is used to calculate the best order size and the best time to order.

    *   A par stock is the number of items that a buyer feels must be on hand to maintain a continuing supply of the item from one delivery date to the next.

    *   Typically, a buyer subtracts what is on hand from the par stock number, then orders that amount along with any additional amount necessary to cover anticipated special events or increased sales volume.

    *   While the par stock approach is at best a trial-and-error approach to inventory management, it works effectively in the hospitality industry.

3. The **Levinson approach** is a more complicated approach that requires systemic, computerized inventory management. In general, this approach calls for buyers to do the following:

    *   Forecast both the expected total number of customers and popularity indexes for each menu item.

    *   Calculate the **portion factor (PF)** by dividing the unit of measurement (sixteen ounces for pounds) by the serving size of an item.

    *   Next, find the **portion divider (PD)** for each ingredient by multiplying the portion factor by the ingredient's edible-yield percentage.

- To calculate order sizes for each item, divide the number of customers expected to consume the ingredient by the portion divider for that ingredient.
- Adjust order size to take into account stock on hand and anticipated special events or increased sales volume.
- Some buyers use the par stock method for normal operation and the Levinson approach for special events.

4. In large, multiunit foodservice companies where inventory value reaches multimillion-dollar levels, a more formal, **theoretical approach** to purchasing and inventory control is often used to justify major spending and purchasing systems.
   - With the theoretical approach, correct order size is influenced by **storage cost** (also known as "carrying cost") and the **ordering cost**.
   - Experts estimate that storage costs run from ten percent to twenty-five percent of an inventory's value.
   - Ordering costs reflect all the expenses associated with processing and receiving an order.
   - Theoretically, there is one optimal order size where the storage cost equals the ordering cost.
   - Several industries have adopted the **economic order quantity** (**EOQ**) formula as a reference to identify the relevant costs involved in optimal order sizes.
   - Since there is a lag time between the time an order is placed and the time it arrives, a buyer must reduce the supply of each item to some level greater than zero to avoid running out of inventory. This level is called the **safety stock** or the **reorder point** (**ROP**).
   - Operations that strive to run out of inventory precisely when the next order arrives are practicing "**just-in-time**" (**JIT**) inventory management.

5. While the basic overall problem with the theoretical method is the need for certain assumptions and estimates, there are several additional variables that detract from its usefulness:
   - Usage rates typically vary from day to day.
   - Storage and ordering costs can vary.
   - The impact of stockouts is difficult to assess.
   - The inability to control delivery times makes lead times less predictable.
   - It is often difficult to determine which items should be considered for EOQ and ROP.
   - Buyer's EOQ differs from supplier's EOQ, increasing the likelihood of incomplete orders.
   - The fact that items with a limited supply (i.e., vintage wines) are often ordered in larger quantities goes against EOQ and ROP concepts.

- EOQ assumes the adequacy of storage facilities and that products ordered will be used before they spoil.

6. Benefits of the theoretical approach include:

   - Forces buyers to consider a number of variables that can easily lead to more favorable profit performance

   - Verifies that there is a range or order sizes in which the total cost per year does not vary dramatically

Chapter 9 Exercises

1. Abigail, the owner/operator of Abigail's Inn, uses the par stock approach to purchasing. She has determined that her operation's par stock for tomato sauce is 8 cases. Before placing an order for more, she notes that there are 2 cases left. ½ case will be used today, and she needs 3 more cases for an upcoming special event. How many cases should she order?

_____

L.O. 9.1

2. Dean's restaurant estimates that next week, 20% of its 2,240 customers will order salmon. One portion is 6 ounces, and 1 pound yields 70%.

   a. How many customers are expected to order salmon?

   _____

   b. Using the Levinson approach, what is the portion factor for salmon?

   _____

   c. What is the portion divider for salmon?

   _____

   d. What is the order size of salmon needed to fulfill production needs?

   _____

L.O. 9.1

3. Irene, the buyer for a small chain of restaurants, uses the Levinson approach to purchasing. Given the following data, compute the number of raw pounds she will need to order of each ingredient for a special event for 600 people.

Ingredient	Serving size	Edible yield (%)
Chicken	10 ounces	75%
Spinach, frozen, chopped	5 ounces	100%
Potatoes	4 ounces	70%

Number of pounds needed:_____

L.O. 9.1

4. Leo, purchaser for a hotel, uses a variation of the Levinson approach for the hotel's liquor purchases. Given the following data, compute the number of liters he will need to serve 300 customers.

Ingredient	Serving size	Servable yield (%)
Scotch	50 milliliters	90%
Gin	60 milliliters	95%

Number of liters needed:_____

L.O. 9.1

5. Rebecca, the buyer for a sports stadium, uses a theoretical approach to purchasing. The stadium uses 400 cases of nacho cheese sauce per year. Ordering cost per order is $5.00, and annual storage cost is 20% of the value of the cheese. The cost of the cheese is $9.50 per case. What is the economic order quantity in dollars? In units? What is the annual total cost associated with this order size?

- _____

- _____

- _____

L.O. 9.1

6. Explain at least two variables that detract from the usefulness of the theoretical approach?

- _____

  _____

- _____

  _____

L.O. 9.2

Chapter 9 Check-in

1. How many times should the food inventory in a quick-service restaurant generally turn over?

    A. 3 times per week
    B. 4 times per week
    C. 5 times per week
    D. 7 times per week

    L.O. 9.1

2. If Joshua needs 5 cases of baked beans on hand to last between orders, there are 2 ½ cases left on the morning he is going to place the order, ½ case will be used that day, and the par stock is 8, how many cases should Joshua order?

    A. 4 cases
    B. 5 cases
    C. 6 cases
    D. 7 cases

    L.O. 9.1

3. When ordering using the par stock approach, a buyer should subtract what is on hand from the

    A. EP cost.
    B. safety stock.
    C. par stock.
    D. ROP.

    L.O. 9.1

4. Buyers using the Levinson approach try to order most merchandise on a

    A. daily basis.
    B. weekly basis.
    C. monthly basis.
    D. annual basis.

    L.O. 9.1

5. If Luigi's sold 800 menu items for the week and 140 of them were baked spaghetti, what is the popularity index for that item?

    A. 5.7%
    B. 7.1%
    C. 11.6%
    D. 17.5%

    L.O. 9.1

6. If the edible yield for 8 ounces of potatoes is 70%, what is the order size, in raw pounds, needed to serve 600 people?

    A. 300 pounds
    B. 392 pounds
    C. 420 pounds
    D. 429 pounds

    L.O. 9.1

7. The largest element of the storage cost in the theoretical approach is the

    A. ordering cost.
    B. capital cost.
    C. stockout cost.
    D. carrying cost.

    L.O. 9.1

8. The point at which the storage-cost curve intersects the ordering-cost curve is the

    A. total cost.
    B. optimal order size.
    C. reorder point.
    D. edible-yield percentage.

    L.O. 9.1

9. Which of the following is problematic for buyers who use the theoretical approach?

    A. Stockout costs are difficult to assess.
    B. Usage rates follow a predictable pattern.
    C. Suppliers rarely, if ever, run out of items.
    D. The EOQ assumes that the buyer has adequate production capabilities.

L.O. 9.2

10. Users of the theoretical approach need not worry if estimates are a little off because

    A. computer technology makes it more feasible to monitor EOQs and ROPs.
    B. the range of order sizes for the total annual cost does not vary dramatically.
    C. spoilage is not a big problem.
    D. lead times are somewhat predictable.

L.O. 9.2

CHAPTER 10

Learning Objectives

After reading this chapter, you should be able to:

10.1   Explain how purchase prices influence buyers.

10.2   Describe how suppliers determine their purchase prices.

10.3   Identify methods that buyers employ to reduce purchase prices.

10.4   Calculate cost information, including edible portion cost, servable portion cost, and standard cost.

10.5   Evaluate the advantage of an opportunity buy.

Chapter 10 Study Outline

1. **Optimal price** represents the lowest EP cost consistent with optimal value of a product, service, furnishing, or piece of equipment.
    *   *EP cost = AP price ÷ Edible yield percentage.*
2. AP prices influence buyers in many ways:
    *   At the extreme ends of the spectrum, some buyers shop entirely on the basis of purchase price, while others are concerned only with quality and supplier services. Most buyers fall somewhere in between.
    *   New buyers tend to overrate AP prices in looking at the overall value of a product or service.
    *   While quality is linked to price, quality often fails to keep pace with rising AP prices at the higher end of the market.
    *   The fact that the demands of a hospitality operation's customers tend to translate into the demands that its buyer will have with suppliers is known as a "derived demand." As a result, suppliers often analyze an operation's customers to see if prices are likely to be a secondary concern.
    *   Price becomes less important if the supplier is the exclusive distributor of an item.
    *   Buyers who demand to see an itemized bill (i.e., a bill that breaks out the item's cost from its delivery and other service costs) are almost certainly price conscious.

- The greater an item's cost is to an operation's overall expenses, the more price conscious the buyer tends to become.
- Buyers on a materials budget often become more price conscious toward the end of the budget cycle.

3. Suppliers use at least four general methods to determine AP prices:
   - **Supplier's costs** are added into AP prices, along with a predetermined profit markup. Suppliers sometimes rely on the numerical shorthand known as "rules" to create these markups; the AP price for an item with a "rule of three," for example, would be the item's cost multiplied by three.
   - **Supply and demand** can have a great effect on AP prices, especially perishable foods, commodities, and other raw items entering the channel of distribution.
   - **Competitive pressures** prompt suppliers to provide services that will differentiate their operation. In turn, the perceived value of these services to a supplier's customers can often justify higher AP prices than a competitor may charge—even for products that are essentially the same.
   - **Buyer pricing** comes about when suppliers "assist" buyers in developing specs, or when the buyer consistently engages in "panic" buying. Both circumstances generally lead buyers to overpay for products and services.

4. Buyers seeks to lower AP price by:
   - Paying less for a product yet keeping the same quality and supplier services
   - Effectively using make-or-buy analysis
   - Providing one's own services and/or economic values
   - Shopping around frequently
   - Lowering quality standards (though such actions risk tarnishing the operation's image with customers)
   - Placing blanket orders on miscellaneous low-cost items
   - Improving negotiations with suppliers
   - Using substitutes as a means of lowering the total cost of an operation
   - Taking advantage of cash discounts or "cash rebates"
   - Hedging prices so that the AP price remains stable over a longer period of time
   - Using economical packaging, including large-volume packs whenever available
   - Accepting deliveries at odd hours, especially when coordinated with several different suppliers
   - Participating in co-op purchasing
   - Using cost-plus purchasing, in which a supplier agrees that the AP price is equal to cost plus an agreed-upon profit markup
   - Taking advantage of promotional discounts

- Participating in exchange bartering (experts suggest this should only represent ten percent to fifteen percent of total sales volume.)
- Taking advantage of suppliers' introductory offers
- Reevaluating EP costs

5. To calculate the **standard cost** of a menu item, find the EP cost of all the individual products that go into the menu item, and then add them together.
   - **Suggested menu price** = Standard cost ÷ Target product cost %.

6. Buyers can reduce their AP prices dramatically by taking advantage of **opportunity buys**.

7. Suppliers offer opportunity buys for a variety of reasons:
   - As quantity discounts on large purchases of one item
   - As volume discounts for large purchases of several items
   - As an incentive to move either unsalable items or items close to their expiration dates
   - As a way to pass on their own savings to good customers
   - As a way to bring in cash quickly
   - As a way to break into a new market
   - As a way to introduce a new product to the market

8. Buyers must first evaluate the quantitative factors of an opportunity buy.
   - To evaluate an opportunity buy, buyers often divide the savings in dollars by the cost of the additional amount of items that need to be purchased to get the savings. This number is adjusted annually, and then is compared to a cutoff percentage rate, usually a rate that represents the storage cost.
   - Often management sets a high cutoff percentage rate, so that any figures that exceed it are indeed good buys.
   - The cutoff percentage rate should be different for items that have different storage costs.

9. If the numbers on an opportunity buy work, buyers then ask themselves a series of qualitative questions, including:
   - Is the quality of the opportunity buy comparable to what is currently used?
   - What is the probability that its AP price will soon decrease?
   - Do we have both sufficient cash reserves and storage facilities?
   - What is the storage life of the item(s)?
   - What will be the effect of the buy on current storage costs?
   - How might the buy impact our current supplier (especially if the buy comes from a new supplier)?
   - Would there be a big difference in supplier services?

- Is there any possibility that the goods have been illegally obtained, lack official government inspection, or come from an unlicensed distributor?
- Is the supplier going through bankruptcy, resulting in the goods actually belonging to creditors?
- Would the purchase violate local health codes relating to sales by unapproved vendors?
- If buying used items, will they last as long as new items most likely would?

Chapter 10 Exercises

1. Put a check mark next to each statement that accurately describes how AP prices influence buyers.

_____a. A buyer's demand is derived from the ultimate customer's demand.

_____b. AP prices of meat products are usually scrutinized closely.

_____c. Buyers who seek an itemized bill are not price conscious.

_____d. Novice buyers tend to put too much emphasis on AP prices.

_____e. When an operation's customers are price conscious, price is of secondary importance.

_____f. Buyers who operate on a tight materials budget are more price conscious when the budget period begins its cycle than they would ordinarily be.

_____g. Price usually follows quality.

L.O. 10.1

2. Name and describe the four methods that suppliers use in determining AP prices.

- _____

_____

- _____

_____

- _____

_____

- _____

_____

L.O. 10.2

3. List one advantage and one disadvantage of doing each of the following to decrease AP price:

a. Conducting a make-or-buy analysis

_____

_____

b. Shopping around more frequently

_____

_____

c. Using blanket orders

_____

_____

d. Carrying substitute products

_____

_____

e. Hedging

_____

_____

f. Using odd-hours deliveries

_____

_____

g. Using promotional discounts

_____

_____

h. Using introductory offers

_____

_____

L.O. 10.3

4. Peter is trying to establish a price for the Grand Corned Beef Platter, a new item appear on The Grand Bar & Grill's menu next month. Information about the item is as follows:

Ingredient	Edible yield (%)	Serving size	AP price per pound/kilogram
Cooked corned beef round	40%	8 ounces	$2.55 per pounds
Frozen leaf spinach	100%	90 grams	$3.05 per kilogram
Potatoes	75%	4 ounces	$0.90 per pound

a. What is each ingredient's EP cost?

_____

_____

_____

b. What is the menu item's standard cost?

_____

c. If Peter wants the food cost of the corned beef dinner item to be 26% of its menu price, what should the menu price be?

_____

L.O. 10.4

5. Danny, the buyer for Chili Pepper, usually purchases 400 cases of canned tomatoes once a month. The AP price is $6.00 per case. Danny has an opportunity to purchase a two-month supply for $5.90 per case. His ordering cost for each order is $33.00. Storage costs are 2% per month. Should Danny buy a two-month supply of canned tomatoes? Explain your answer.

_____

_____

_____

L.O. 10.5

Chapter 10 Check-in

1. The practice of shopping entirely on the basis of AP price can be successful if
   A. inflation is low.
   B. buyers can get one supplier to quote acceptable AP prices.
   C. buyers know exactly what they want in terms of quality and supplier services.
   D. price does not follow quality.
   L.O. 10.1

2. Suppliers should conduct an analysis of their customers' customers because the amount they sell to hospitality firms is heavily influenced by
   A. derived demand.
   B. changing preferences.
   C. local trends.
   D. buyer profiles.
   L.O. 10.1

3. A supplier that uses a "rule of three" determines AP prices based on
   A. supply and demand.
   B. buyer pricing.
   C. competitors' prices.
   D. its costs.
   L.O. 10.2

4. The most common way to reduce the effect of supply and demand on prices is to
   A. apply a certain profit markup to product cost.
   B. differentiate products.
   C. encourage "panic buying."
   D. measure buyer reaction to AP prices.
   L.O. 10.2

5. When seeking a lower AP price, a buyer's emphasis should be on
   A. increasing overall value.
   B. obtaining favorable supplier services.
   C. ensuring that a purchased product fulfills its intended use.
   D. decreasing "line-item purchasing."
   L.O. 10.3

6. Maintaining a specific AP price is the primary aim in
   A. negotiation.
   B. hedging.
   C. placing blanket orders.
   D. obtaining cash discounts.
   L.O. 10.3

7. While the practice of _____ is frequently employed in the hospitality industry, its use should be kept to 10–15% of total sales volume.
   A. bartering
   B. backdoor selling
   C. co-op purchasing
   D. introductory offers
   L.O. 10.3

8. The servable portion cost of a 50-milliliter serving of scotch with a servable yield of 95% and an AP price of $9.10 per liter is
   A. $0.19.
   B. $0.48.
   C. $0.72.
   D. $0.91.
   L.O. 10.4

9. The EP costs for each component of a chicken dinner menu item are as follows:

Chicken $3.98
Beans $0.12
Potatoes $0.41

If the food cost percentage of the menu item is to be 25% of its menu price, a suggested menu price might be

A. $4.50.
B. $7.95.
C. $11.50.
D. $17.99.

L.O. 10.4

10. A buyer will usually purchase an additional one-month's supply of a product if the supplier discounts the AP price by

A. 2–3%.
B. 3–4%.
C. 4–5%.
D. 5–6%.

L.O. 10.5

CHAPTER 11

Learning Objectives

After reading this chapter, you should be able to:

11.1   Identify the major objective of a payment policy.

11.2   Explain the costs of paying sooner than necessary and of paying too late.

11.3   Compare the bill-paying procedures that can be employed by hospitality operators.

Chapter 11 Study Outline

1. The objectives of cash management are to keep money as long as possible, pay bills at the correct time, and collect monies due as fast as possible.

    *   The buyer or accountant must balance the costs of paying money too early with the potential ill will created among suppliers who must wait too long for payment.

2. The major costs of paying bills too early include losing potential interest income from the cash (a problem for larger operations) or becoming cash starved (a problem for smaller operations).

3. The costs of paying too late include damaging credit ratings, jeopardizing future credit potential, and incurring penalty charges.

4. The best payment policy is one that allows an operation to keep its money as long as possible, unless there is an incentive to pay early.

    *   Most suppliers expect a **cash-on-delivery**, or **COD payment** unless the buyer's operation has established credit, in which case most suppliers allow balances to be paid in full within thirty days without incurring late penalties.

    *   While periodic payment schedules may not allow small hospitality operations to keep their money as long as they might like, systemizing their payments so that everything gets paid once a week allows them to establish good credit.

5. Bill-paying procedures can include one or several forms:

    *   **Paid-outs**, in which an operation directly pays for a COD delivery by giving the driver either cash or a prepared check, are a common method of payment among small operations.

- **Invoices on account** allow operations to pay for expenses at the end of the credit period. Suppliers typically submit a statement at the end of the credit period, and the hospitality operation checks these statements against its invoice copies/credit slips that were generated when the goods/services were delivered/rendered.
- **Credit card payments** allow even relatively new hospitality operations to have credit terms, while providing suppliers with a secure payment. At the end of the credit period, the credit card company handles the billing rather than the supplier.
- For a fee, a **bill-paying service** takes money that a hospitality operation has deposited into an escrow account and uses it to pay the operation's accounts payable.
- Large operations can earn considerable income just by keeping track of a supplier's **cash discount period** (usually ten days), then paying the bill at the last possible moment.
- While discounts may be attractive for larger operations, they sometimes cause problems, such as distorting the real cost of purchases; interfering with the firm's accounts-payable schedule; staying with a supplier who regularly discounts too long; forcing a firm to borrow cash; and causing disputes with suppliers over whether the cash discount period should be extended when replacement goods are involved.

Chapter 11 Exercises

1. What are the basic principles of cash management?

_____

_____

_____

L.O. 11.1

2. Why should hospitality operations avoid paying bills sooner than necessary?

_____

_____

_____

L.O. 11.2

3. Why should hospitality operations avoid paying bills late?

_____

_____

_____

L.O. 11.2

4. Indicate whether each of the following is associated with paid-outs (P), invoices on account (I), credit card payments (C), or bill-paying services (B).

_____a. Receiver pays the delivery driver.

_____b. Suppliers must pay a fee to the company handling the billing.

_____c. Operations deposit money into an escrow account.

_____d. Hospitality operations must pay a fee to the bill-paying entity, but they enjoy an extra margin of security.

_____e. Most suppliers will agree to the procedures as long as the amount of money involved is not too large.

_____f. Suppliers enjoy administrative savings because they do not handle a large amount of the paperwork.

_____g. At the end of the credit period, the operation receives a statement listing all amounts delivered during the period.

_____h. Operation sends the supplier a check after reconciling the supplier's statement with its own records.

L.O. 11.3

Chapter 11 Check-in

1. Buyers usually have little influence on their company's payment procedures unless they are
   A. full-time employees.
   B. CPAs.
   C. cash starved.
   D. the owners who pay the bills.
   L.O. 11.1

2. Which of the following is a tenet of cash management?
   A. Pay bills as quickly as possible.
   B. Collect monies due on a weekly basis.
   C. Seek out financial incentives for paying earlier than usual.
   D. Keep money as long as possible.
   L.O. 11.1

3. If an operation pays $35,000 today instead of one week from today, and the bank handling its money pays 5% simple interest per year on deposits, how much money will the operation lose?
   A. $33.65
   B. $70.00
   C. $1,231.75
   D. $1,750.00
   L.O. 11.2

4. Most hospitality firms do not typically invest money because
   A. the market is too risky.
   B. few firms have cash balances large enough to justify the time and effort needed to keep cash invested productively.
   C. doing so can leave them cash starved and vulnerable to excessive financial risks.
   D. they rarely earn annual profits.
   L.O. 11.2

5. An operation can damage its credit ratings by
   A. making partial payments.
   B. paying on a cash-on-delivery basis.
   C. paying too late.
   D. buying only from suppliers who provide low-quality merchandise.
   L.O. 11.2

6. Hospitality operations that have established credit will usually
   A. pay COD.
   B. delay paying their bills.
   C. be put on a monthly credit-term period.
   D. incur substantial interest charges.
   L.O. 11.3

7. How long is the credit-term period usually sought by large hospitality firms?
   A. Ten days
   B. Twenty-five days
   C. Thirty days
   D. Forty-five days
   L.O. 11.3

8. The paid-out method of bill paying emphasizes which of the following?

   A. Paying cash on delivery
   B. Avoiding check-printing costs and other bank charges
   C. Paying at the end of the credit period
   D. Negotiating product prices

L.O. 11.3

9. After reconciling a supplier's statement with a hospitality operation's own records, the operation sends the supplier a check under which bill-paying method?

   A. Credit card payments
   B. Paid-outs
   C. Bill-paying service
   D. Invoices on account

L.O. 11.3

10. Some hospitality operations authorize a bill-paying service to pay their accounts payable by using money deposited in a(n)

   A. escrow account.
   B. checking account.
   C. money market account.
   D. credit account.

L.O. 11.3

CHAPTER 12

THE OPTIMAL SUPPLIER

Learning Objectives

After reading this chapter, you should be able to:

12.1   Determine a buying plan by selecting a single supplier or bid buying.

12.2   Explain additional criteria used when choosing suppliers.

12.3   Describe the relationship between suppliers and buyers.

12.4   Describe the relationship between salespersons and buyers.

12.5   Identify ways to evaluate the performance of salespersons and suppliers.

Chapter 12 Study Outline

1. Determining the optimal supplier requires developing a list of possible suppliers.

    *   The list should be trimmed by examining each supplier's product quality, AP price, and services.

    *   Buyers should consider which type of procurement policies might work best for them, then find suppliers who can accommodate these policies.

2. In the foodservice industry, there are two basic buying plans:

    *   Buyer selects a supplier first, and they work together to meet the buyer's needs. Smaller operations, with their time and personnel constraints, often choose this option.

    *   Buyer prepares detailed specs for the items needed and then uses bid-buying procedures.

3. Buyers should evaluate several variables when developing a list of acceptable suppliers. They include:

    *   **Cost-plus purchasing** is especially attractive for larger operations since it tends to lower AP prices.

    *   **One-stop shopping** can greatly simplify ordering/receiving processes, but it also can reduce flexibility and end up costing more in the long run.

- **Stockless purchasing** involves postponing delivery of a portion of an order until it is need at a later date. Limited-supply items and items that look to see a sharp rise in AP prices are often purchased this way.

- The **cash-and-carry** option, also known as "will-call purchasing," requires a hospitality operation to provide its own delivery of goods. It is a useful option for operations such as off-premise caterers, whose unpredictable business makes it difficult for them to meet suppliers' regular delivery requirements.

- **Standing orders** allow suppliers such as dairy or bread distributors to deliver just enough stock to bring the buyer's stock up to par.

- **Use of technology**—such as e-procurement.

- **Co-op purchasing** is experiencing renewed popularity, thanks to the rise of aggregate purchasing companies that use the Internet to streamline the process for buyers.

- Local merchant wholesalers versus national sources

- **Delivery schedules** are rarely optimal from an operation's standpoint, but a supplier who matches preferred delivery times should be looked at more closely.

- Convenient **ordering procedures** give suppliers a competitive edge.

- Generous **credit terms** are especially attractive to many hospitality operations.

- **Minimum order requirements** must be met to avoid additional delivery charges.

- Suppliers try to offer a reasonable **variety of merchandise**, with choices from several different grades, brand names, and/or packers' brands.

- The shorter the **lead time** on an order, the more convenient it is for the buyer.

- **Free samples** from suppliers can increase product awareness and entice large accounts, but some buyers feel such samples may compromise their purchasing independence.

- A supplier's **returns policy** should be as flexible as possible.

- **Reciprocal buying** is the idea of "you buy from me, and I'll buy from you."

- A buyer's **willingness to barter** must be linked to the supplier's desires to accommodate this request.

- A supplier's reluctance to **cooperate in bid procedures** makes him or her a poor match for a bid buyer.

- The **size** of a supplier's company and the number of years it has been in business are both factors that buyers consider.

- Buyers usually avoid suppliers who have a high **number of back orders**, and instead look for those who can claim very high "fill rates."

- Buyers appreciate suppliers who have a good **substitution capability**—the ability to secure the products necessary to complete an order.

- While not a common practice today, some suppliers may still have **buyout policies**, in which they agree to purchase the existing stock of a competitor's product so the buyer can start purchasing their product immediately.

- Suppliers that use **inadequate facilities** or poorly repaired delivery vehicles can easily harm product quality and should therefore be avoided.

- Many suppliers are unwilling or unable to provide **long-term contracts** for AP prices and/or product availability.

- Whereas all buyers want a discounted **case price** on the products they buy, smaller operations often do not use product quickly enough to justify large purchases. Such buyers often look for suppliers who are willing to "bust" a case, offering a partial case at the discounted price.

- **Bonded suppliers** carry insurance that protects the buyer's operation from the cost of any damage that the supplier's product might inflict on that operation or its property. Working with a supplier who is not bonded is extremely risky.

- **Consulting services** that go beyond the product expertise of most suppliers can be valuable to a buyer who is purchasing large equipment that may require building permits and contractors to install.

- While **deposits** are often required for items such as soda-pop containers or beer kegs, the cost of these deposits should not be burdensome. If a supplier seems overly demanding, other suppliers should be sought.

- **Willingness to sell storage** can be a valuable supplier service for buyers, but they should inquire about storage fees and minimum purchase requirements beforehand.

- Buyers often must decide if they should work with **suppliers who own hospitality operations** themselves, weighing the potential conflict of buying from a competitor against the benefits that come in dealing with a supplier who truly understands the buyer's side of the business and provides good service accordingly.

- Some buyers prefer to work with **socially responsible suppliers**.

- Buyers look to friends and associates in the industry to provide them with **references** about a supplier's integrity and dependability.

- According to most buyer surveys, buyers tend to choose their suppliers by product quality first, supplier services second, and AP prices as their third and final concern.

4. The duties of supply-house officers include:

- Setting the tone of the business
- Setting overall sales strategies
- Sponsoring product and market research, especially "buyer fact sheets"
- Training sales staff
- Keeping their salespeople's promises

5. Since salespersons are a hospitality operation's main supplier contact, buyers should be aware that a salesperson's goals during his or her first sales call might include one or more of the following:

    - Make a slight attempt at backdoor selling with kitchen or bar staff.
    - Use free samples as a way to interest or obligate buyers
    - Establish a justification for their presence
    - Attempt to talk buyers away from their current supplier(s)
    - Start an ongoing business relationship by creating a reason to return

6. Salespersons regularly practice "relationship marketing," in which they work to gain even a small portion of a buyer's business. This initial sale, in turn, justifies future visits, during which they pursue their main objective: developing the customer into a regular account.

    - Buyers must weigh the time they spend meeting with salespersons against the product information they might not otherwise gain were they to shut out most salespersons.
    - While the selling relationship is not necessarily adversarial, buyers should learn about sales tactics, strategies, and procedures so they can more effectively negotiate with salespersons.

7. Buyers should periodically evaluate suppliers and their salespersons after a business relationship has been established, and reward or discipline them accordingly.

    - The ultimate reward is to become a house account for the supplier, while the ultimate discipline is to switch to another supplier.
    - Buyers should evaluate suppliers and salespersons on their ability to provide consistent quality and services.
    - A supplier or salesperson whose consistency has slipped should be given a chance to improve their performance, largely because "firing" the supplier may leave the buyer with poorer supply choices.
    - While a supplier who takes good care of a buyer's needs deserves that buyer's loyalty, the buyer's obligation to the operation requires him/her occasionally to examine alternate suppliers and to make a switch if necessary.

Chapter 12 Exercises

1. What are the two basic buying plans used in the hospitality industry?

    - _____

    - _____

L.O. 12.1

2. What is the difference between a fixed bid and a daily bid?

_____

_____

_____

L.O. 12.1

3. Match the following descriptions with the term or concept it describes below.

_____(1) Buyer purchases a large amount of product but arranges for the supplier to store and deliver it as needed.

_____(2) "You buy from me, I'll buy from you."

_____(3) Buyer is charged for whatever the supplier pays plus an agreed-upon mark-up percentage.

_____(4) Banding together of several small operators in order to consolidate their buying power

_____(5) Supplier who has adequate insurance coverage

_____(6) Procedure in which a buyer provides his or her own deliveries

_____(7) Supplier who wants your business agrees to buy existing stock of competitors' merchandise.

_____(8) Limiting the number of suppliers to a single supplier for as many products as possible

_____(9) Order placed with a supplier who repeatedly delivers just enough to bring the buyer's stock level up to par

_____(10) Buyer prepares specs for items needed and then uses bid-buying procedures.

_____(11) System used by suppliers to sell their products that eliminates the need for buyers to install proprietary software on their computers

_____(12) Number of items delivered divided by the number ordered

a. Buying plan
b. Cash-and-carry
c. Bonded supplier
d. Cost-plus purchasing
e. Standing order
f. Buyout policy
g. Stockless purchasing
h. Reciprocal buying
i. One-stop shopping
j. Co-op purchasing
k. Fill rate
l. E-marketplace

L.O. 12.2

4. Name three major activities of the top management of a supply house.

- _____

- _____

- _____

L.O. 12.3

5. Why might a salesperson be willing to take a very small order from a buyer?

_____

_____

_____

L.O. 12.4

6. When a hospitality operation evaluates a supplier, what is the ultimate discipline it can impose? The ultimate reward it can give?

_____

_____

_____

L.O. 12.5

Chapter 12 Check-in

1. The first step in determining the optimal supplier is to
   A. determine the hospitality operation's needs.
   B. examine suppliers' product quality, AP price, and services.
   C. compile a list of all possible suppliers.
   D. consider the best type of procurement policy for the hospitality operation.
   L.O. 12.1

2. A buyer who wants to purchase large quantities of products over a reasonably long period of time will most likely
   A. use a daily bid.
   B. work together with a supplier to meet the buyer's needs.
   C. employ a fixed bid.
   D. participate in one-stop shopping.
   L.O. 12.1

3. A daily bid is often used for purchasing
   A. fresh produce.
   B. canned goods.
   C. large amounts.
   D. small amounts.
   L.O. 12.1

4. Suppliers who offer numerous services and, as a result, have high AP prices frequently
   A. present opportunity buys.
   B. balk at bid buying.
   C. employ cost-plus pricing.
   D. sell storage to buyers.
   L.O. 12.3

5. A buyer who prefers to purchase a large amount of product and then take delivery of the entire shipment at one time is practicing
   A. stockless purchasing.
   B. reciprocal buying.
   C. forward buying.
   D. cash-and-carry.
   L.O. 12.2

6. Most suppliers who want to stay competitive are considering some form of
   A. co-op purchasing.
   B. installment payment procedure.
   C. bartering.
   D. e-procurement.
   L.O. 12.2

7. Which of the following is an example of a socially responsible supplier?
   A. Exhibits little integrity or overall dependability
   B. Carries products whose processing causes damage to the Earth's resources
   C. Deals with minority-owned subcontractors
   D. Buys out an operation's existing stock so that the operation can begin to use new merchandise immediately
   L.O. 12.2

8. What is the ultimate reward that a buyer can offer a supplier who has consistently met the buyer's quality and service needs?

   A. The buyer can adopt a policy of infrequently meeting with other suppliers.
   B. The buyer should always reserve the right to switch suppliers.
   C. The buyer can shift more of his/her business over to the deserving supplier.
   D. The buyer can agree to become a house account of the supplier.

   L.O. 12.5

9. A full-time buyer for a large operation is expected to spend a good deal of time with

   A. other department heads.
   B. salespeople.
   C. accountants.
   D. supply-house officers.

   L.O. 12.4

10. The main objective of salespeople is to

    A. provide a hospitality customer with satisfaction.
    B. develop good trade relations in the industry.
    C. practice relationship marketing.
    D. convert a hospitality operation into a regular customer.

    L.O. 12.4

CHAPTER 13

TYPICAL ORDERING PROCEDURES

Learning Objectives

After reading this chapter, you should be able to:

13.1 Explain the use of a purchase requisition.

13.2 Describe the elements of a purchase order and its use.

13.3 Recognize methods to streamline the ordering process.

Chapter 13 Study Outline

1. **Purchase requisitions** are forms created by department heads that request an operation's buyer to purchase items or services that the buyer would not regularly order.

2. Before placing an order, buyers determine the appropriate order size by using either the par stock or Levinson approach to ordering.

3. Ordering procedures vary, but may include: giving a verbal order to a salesperson in person, writing down an order and then faxing it to a supplier, sending it to a salesperson as an e-mail attachment, or ordering directly through a supplier's e-procurement Web site.

   - Management usually decides what ordering procedure will be used, unless the supplier has a specific requirement.

4. **Purchase orders**, or **POs**, are requests for a supplier to deliver items at a desired time.

   - POs generally include the following: order date, transportation requirements, packaging instructions, desired receiving date, quantity desired, item type, unit size, unit price, and extended price (number of units multiplied by unit price).

   - Typically, copies of the PO go to the supplier, the receiving clerk, and the buyer.

   - A **limited purchase order**, or **LPO**, can control the cost and quality of merchandise by restricting the overall amount that a buyer can purchase on a particular PO form.

   - Ultimately, POs are simply a means for controlling products and services.

   - While **change orders**—alterations to an original PO made by the buyer—happen from time to time, they should be avoided, since the PO is technically a legally binding contract.

- Buyers will often **expedite** a large or crucial order; that is, they will contact the supplier frequently to ensure products and services arrive at the right time and in the right condition.

5. Methods to help streamline the ordering procedure include:

- Using **blanket orders**—the purchase of large amounts of miscellaneous items at the same time—can save ordering costs without largely impacting storage costs.
- Creating a **purchase order draft system**, whereby the operation prepays for an order with either a check or credit card, can reduce paperwork and result in a cash discount from the supplier.
- Printed or Web-based **suppliers' forms** often reduce a buyer's paperwork costs.
- **Standing orders** minimize ordering costs by eliminating the need to prepare POs.
- **Computerization** and e-procurement applications represent tremendous savings for both the supplier and the buyer.

Chapter 13 Exercises

As buyer for Holiday Hotel's restaurants, lounges, and room service, Rebecca is preparing to place weekly orders for food and beverages.

1. If the bar manager would like to test the popularity of a new malt beverage, what form would she most likely need to fill out and submit to Rebecca?

_____

L.O. 13.1

2. Describe at least two ways Rebecca could place her orders with her suppliers.

- _____

- _____

L.O. 13.2

3. What type of information should Rebecca include on all of her purchase orders?

_____

_____

_____

L.O. 13.2

4. Holiday Hotel typically requires the preparation of three copies of every purchase order.

    a. To whom will each copy go?

    _____

    _____

    _____

    b. Why is the decision on how many copies to use an important one?

    _____

    _____

    _____

L.O. 13.2

5. Rebecca is preparing for a banquet for five hundred people in Holiday Hotel's grand ballroom. In anticipation of the banquet, she calls her supplier to check on the five hundred steaks and seafood items that have been ordered. What is Rebecca's effort to ensure that the food arrives at the right time and in an acceptable condition called?

    _____

L.O. 13.2

6. Rebecca is reexamining the ordering procedure used at Holiday Hotel. Name three ways that she can streamline the procedure.

    • _____

    • _____

    • _____

L.O. 13.3

Chapter 13 Check-in

1. The buyer's responsibilities end when
    A. products have been received.
    B. orders have been placed.
    C. products have been accepted with a signature.
    D. products have been turned over to those who will use them.

L.O. 13.1

2. Forms that list items and services needed by particular department heads are called
    A. blanket orders.
    B. change orders.
    C. product requisitions.
    D. purchase requisitions.

L.O. 13.1

3. A purchase requisition typically is used when a manager needs an item that is

    A. not ordered regularly by the buyer.

    B. ordered regularly by the buyer.

    C. ordered on a monthly basis by the buyer.

    D. ordered from a new supplier.

L.O. 13.1

4. Use of a purchase requisition

    A. requires a great deal of paperwork.

    B. relieves a buyer of responsibility for ordering mistakes.

    C. relinquishes control of the use of products and services in the various departments.

    D. eliminates many people from the ordering and decision process.

L.O. 13.1

5. Which order-placement method represents the future of the industry?

    A. Phoning orders into suppliers

    B. Using a Web-based e-procurement application

    C. Sending orders via an e-mail attachment to suppliers

    D. Giving orders to the supplier's salesperson

L.O. 13.2

6. Requesting that a supplier deliver products at a desired time is called a

    A. blanket order.

    B. purchase order.

    C. standing order.

    D. stock requisition.

L.O. 13.2

7. Which of the following typically appears on a purchase order?

    A. Size of the supplier's firm

    B. Packaging instructions

    C. Desired processing

    D. Point of origin

L.O. 13.2

8. How many copies of a purchase order are most commonly prepared?

    A. Three

    B. Five

    C. Six

    D. Eight

L.O. 13.2

9. A purchase order with a check attached to cover the cost of the ordered items

    A. increases the need for clerical work.

    B. includes a large amount of miscellaneous items.

    C. eliminates the need to prepare purchase orders.

    D. is called a purchase order draft system.

L.O. 13.3

10. Which streamlining opportunity drastically reduces the costs associated with paper?

    A. Standing order

    B. Purchase order draft system

    C. E-procurement applications

    D. Blanket orders

L.O. 13.3

CHAPTER 14

TYPICAL RECEIVING PROCEDURES

Learning Objectives

After reading this chapter, you should be able to:

14.1   Explain the objectives of receiving.

14.2   Identify the essentials of effective receiving.

14.3   Describe invoice receiving and other receiving methods.

14.4   Outline additional receiving duties.

14.5   List good receiving practices and methods to reduce receiving costs.

Chapter 14 Study Outline

1. The main objectives of receiving are to ensure that the correct amount and quality of products have been delivered at the correct time with the correct supplier services for the correct EP cost.

   - Since the cycle of control begins once a shipment is accepted, controlling received products and services is another important objective of receiving.

2. Competent personnel, proper receiving equipment, proper receiving facilities, appropriate receiving hours, and copies of all specifications and the purchase order are all needed in effective receiving.

3. The following steps are involved in invoice receiving:

   - Delivery arrives accompanied by an invoice.

   - Invoice is compared to the original purchase order.

   - Delivery is inspected—either by the receiver alone, or in conjunction with appropriate department head who inspects products more closely for quality.

   - Delivery is then accepted or rejected.

   - Rejected merchandise is returned, and a credit memo is received.

   - Accepted merchandise is dated, tagged, and moved to storage.

   - Larger operations may have the receiver complete a receiving sheet to uncover possible errors earlier in the receiving process.

4. Additional receiving duties include dating and pricing all delivered items, creating bar codes, applying meat tags, doing housekeeping tasks, updating AP prices, and backhauling recyclables.

5. Other receiving procedures include:

   - **Standing-order receiving** should be conducted like regular invoice receiving to avoid the quality or quantity of goods from "shrinking."

   - In **blind receiving**, the receiver's invoice does not contain quantities or prices, thereby forcing the receiver to weigh, count, and record the entire order on a "Goods Received without Invoice" slip. By checking this slip against a complete invoice kept with the bookkeeper, management potentially can avoid theft by the receiving clerk. Still, experts generally feel that the practice is archaic, error prone, expensive, and time consuming.

   - While **odd-hours receiving** is not a preferred option, it nonetheless occurs. Efforts should be made to ensure that the person who substitutes for the receiver (typically an assistant manager) has some receiving experience and has a list of proper receiving procedures.

   - **Drop shipments** are deliveries transported by common carrier rather than a delivery person employed by the supplier. While receiving drop shipments is generally the same, any returns not directly the result of driver negligence or error need to be accepted by the receiver and sorted out with the supplier later.

   - While **mailed deliveries** refer to their invoices as "packing slips," the receiving of these packages is generally the same as other goods, with the exception that management, rather than the receiving clerk, generally handles all requests for credit memos.

   - In **COD deliveries**, the receiver is also responsible for paying the delivery agent.

6. Good receiving practices include:

   - Look for excess ice and other packaging that can add dead weight to the item.
   - Inspect the bottom layer as well as the top.
   - Check to see if the package is leaking, swollen, or has other signs indicating possible spoilage.
   - Check labels to make sure items are not past their expiration dates.
   - Do not weigh different types of items together.
   - Avoid having the delivery person help with the receiving procedure.
   - Always watch out for incomplete shipments.
   - Spot-check portioned products for portion weight.
   - Avoid accepting closed shipping containers without first seeing what is inside them.
   - Never accept frozen goods that appear to be refrozen, nor accept fresh goods that appear to have been frozen even once.

- Avoid confusing packers' brand names.
- For fresh food items, give suppliers a shrink allowance.
- Question any product that does not live up to its specs.

7. Field inspectors, night/early-morning deliveries, and one-stop shopping can all help reduce receiving costs.

Chapter 14 Exercises

1. What are the objectives of receiving?

_____

_____

_____

L.O. 14.1

2. Elizabeth is in the process of hiring a receiving clerk for Mexican Hot Spot. Before she begins her search for candidates, she decides to review the essentials needed for good receiving at the Hot Spot.

a. Elizabeth wants to hire a competent receiver. What does she mean by "competent?"

_____

_____

_____

b. What specifically should she train the new receiver to do?

_____

_____

_____

c. What kinds of equipment should Elizabeth provide the new receiver on the job?

_____

_____

_____

d. Elizabeth wants to ensure that the receiving facilities allow the new receiver to perform adequately. What is meant by "facilities?" How can Elizabeth ensure that adequate receiving facilities are set up?

_____

_____

_____

L.O. 14.2

3. Put the following activities for invoice receiving in chronological order. Use the numbers 1 (for the first activity) through 7 (for the last activity).

_____a. Reject part of the order.

_____b. Check for the proper quality.

_____c. Open the receiving area.

_____d. Note a discrepancy with respect to prices on the invoice.

_____e. Check all prices and price extensions.

_____f. Prepare a request for credit memorandum.

_____g. Check for the proper quantities.

L.O. 14.3

4. For each of the following items, indicate the purpose and explain how it is used in the receiving process.

a. Invoice

_____

_____

b. Credit memorandum

_____

_____

c. Pick-up memo

_____

_____

d. Receiving sheet

_____

_____

e. Meat tag

_____

_____

f. Bar code

_____

_____

L.O. 14.3

5. Indicate whether each of the following is true (T) or false (F).

_____a. Receivers tend to "relax" when checking items received on a standing-order basis.

_____b. In invoice receiving, the invoice accompanying the delivery does not contain information about quantity or price.

_____c. Most of the time, an assistant manager receives orders delivered during off-hours.

_____d. When a buyer purchases products from a primary source, he/she usually hires a common carrier to drop-ship the merchandise to the hospitality operation.

_____e. For mailed deliveries, the receiver has the added duty of paying the delivery agent.

L.O. 14.4

6. Name three receiving practices that receivers should follow.

● _____

● _____

● _____

L.O. 14.5

Chapter 14 Check-in

1. In some large firms, additional control of the receiving function is achieved by doing which of the following?

    A. Designating a department head to act as receiver
    B. Placing receiving personnel under the direction of the accounting department
    C. Weighing, measuring, and counting received merchandise
    D. Requiring the receiver to document where delivered items were sent within the operation

    L.O. 14.1

2. To ensure that competent personnel are placed in charge of receiving activity, which of the following is required?

    A. Appropriate training of personnel
    B. Computerized facilities
    C. Proper receiving facilities
    D. Intelligence testing

    L.O. 14.2

3. In smaller operations that do not have extensive receiving equipment, which of the following is a bare minimum?

    A. Calculators
    B. Reliable scales
    C. Bar-code readers
    D. Cutting instruments

    L.O. 14.2

4. One of the biggest benefits of one-stop shopping is that the practice

    A. resolves ambiguities about what was ordered.
    B. reduces the number of hours a receiver must work.
    C. facilitates the receiving process.
    D. provides an added measure of control during the receiving function.

    L.O. 14.2

5. Which price extension will appear on an invoice accompanying a delivery of 90 pounds of T-bone steak with a unit price of $6.98?

    A. $12.89
    B. $77.56
    C. $628.20
    D. $698.00

    L.O. 14.3

6. Which of the following is the best reason for why receivers who find part of a delivery unacceptable will generally avoid returning the entire shipment?

    A. It would reduce storage costs.
    B. It could lead to stockouts.
    C. It would involve the time-consuming task of filling out a request for credit memo.
    D. It could lead to both menu item shortages and unhappy customers.

    L.O. 14.3

7. Many hospitality operations use the "dot system" to

   A. create bar codes.
   B. apply meat tags.
   C. update AP prices.
   D. date and price inventories.

   L.O. 14.4

8. Which of the following alternative receiving methods omits quantities and prices from the receiver's invoice copy?

   A. Standing-order receiving
   B. Blind receiving
   C. Odd-hours receiving
   D. Drop-shipment receiving

   L.O. 14.3

9. When orders are received by mail, the invoices that come with them are usually referred to as

   A. delivery tickets.
   B. bills of lading.
   C. pick-up memos.
   D. packing slips.

   L.O. 14.3

10. A receiving clerk who accepts 20 pounds of fresh lobster when 21 pounds were ordered is giving the supplier a

    A. shrink allowance.
    B. backhaul.
    C. blind receiving credit.
    D. net weight consideration.

    L.O. 14.5

CHAPTER 15

Learning Objectives

After reading this chapter, you should be able to:

15.1   Explain the objectives of storage.

15.2   Identify space, temperature, humidity, and other requirements of proper storage.

15.3   Describe the process of managing storage facilities, including inventory.

15.4   List important storage-management practices for small hospitality operators.

Chapter 15 Study Outline

1. In most operations, the storage function is simply one of the receiver's additional responsibilities, although good control practices often warrant some separation of these responsibilities.

2. The major goal of **storage management** is to prevent loss of merchandise due to theft, pilferage, and spoilage.

    *   Industry experts feel that two to four percent of every sales dollar is lost to employee and customer dishonesty.

    *   Rigid sanitation is a must, both to reduce waste due to spoilage, and to prevent foodborne illness.

3. Proper storage management depends on:

    *   Adequate space—well-managed facilities typically allocate ten to twelve percent of total property to storage

    *   Adequate temperature and humidity—especially important with any potentially hazardous food.

    *   Adequate equipment—including shelving/racks to keep goods off the ground, motorized/nonmotorized trucks to move goods safely, and covered containers to store products before they are put into production

    *   Proximity of storage area to receiving and production areas

    *   Dependable maintenance personnel, either on staff or on call via a contract agreement

    *   Proper security

- Competent personnel who are willing and able to enforce strict storage guidelines, especially issuing rules
- Sufficient time given to personnel to perform necessary storage duties
- Storeroom regulations that dictate who can enter
- Strict issuing procedures

4. To manage storage facilities effectively, storeroom managers should:
   - Classify and organize inventories in a systematic fashion.
   - Keep accurate usage rates for all inventories.
   - Occasionally make emergency runs to prevent stockouts.
   - Keep track of all accumulating surpluses.
   - Dispose items no longer used.
   - Transfer merchandise to other company units, or even competitors, who have requested emergency help.
   - Track all inventories and their corresponding dollar value.

5. Using a **perpetual inventory method** provides a tight degree of control; however, it is of greatest use for a total inventory in hospitality operations in which all departments are integrated into a computerized management information system.

6. A **physical inventory** is an actual counting and valuing of all items in storage and, in some cases, of all items in the in-process inventory.

7. Maintaining tight control over the stock is the most important part of the storeroom manager's job.
   - Control depends upon limiting access to only authorized personnel, and by taking effective and efficient security precautions.
   - Smaller operations that lack a full-time storeroom manager often maintain control by restricting personnel access to closely monitored "working storerooms."
   - A stock requisition is a formal request made by a user for the items needed to carry out necessary tasks.

8. Since a great deal of money, time, and effort is needed to manage inventories adequately, small operators should consider developing a more streamlined approach to storage management.
   - Use one-stop shopping to reduce number of deliveries.
   - Have owner-manager/assistant receive and inspect deliveries.
   - Put expensive items into storage, less expensive items straight into production.
   - Have owner-manager/assistant issue par stocks of expensive items to users at beginning of shifts.
   - Always lock the main storage facilities.

- Have owner-manager/assistant retrieve expensive items from storage if needed during a shift, and have them place any remaining items back into storage at the end of a shift.

- Make sure owner-manager/assistant records the number of expensive items used per shift and provides this information to the bookkeeper.

- Have bookkeeper do "critical-item inventory analysis" to reconcile the amount of items sold to amount of items used.

Chapter 15 Exercises

1. Indicate whether the following activities help buyers control spoilage (S), theft (T), or pilferage (P). Each may control more than one problem.

_____a. Adequate temperature and humidity

_____b. Adequate equipment

_____c. Proximity of storage area to receiving and production areas

_____d. Access to proper maintenance

_____e. Proper security

_____f. Competent personnel to supervise and manage the storage function

_____g. Storeroom regulations

L.O. 15.1, 15.2

2. Employees at a unit of the Pasta Getaway chain have just completed a physical inventory of items in storage at the close of August. They valued their items as follows:

Fresh meat/poultry	$1,440
Fresh produce	966
Other fresh items	819
Frozen meat/poultry	1,410
Other frozen items	922
Canned items	1,048
Other dry-storage items	997
Nonalcoholic beverages	1,264

The unit's accounting office has invoices representing the following purchases for August:

8/3	$3,106
8/10	1,842
8/14	3,466
8/21	3,912
8/25	2,644
8/31	4,298

The restaurant began August with $11,428 in inventory, and sales were $73,500.

a. What is the unit's closing inventory value for August?

_____

b. What is the total value of August purchases?

_____

c. What is the total food cost for August?

_____

d. What is the unit's food cost percentage for August, to the nearest tenth?

_____

L.O. 15.3

3. Name three effective yet economical ways that small operators can manage and control the storage function.

- _____

- _____

- _____

L.O. 15.4

Chapter 15 Check-in

1. One of the basic goals of storage management is to prevent the loss of merchandise due to inventory shrinkage, which is also known as

   A. pilferage.
   B. theft.
   C. spoilage.
   D. turnover.

   L.O. 15.1

2. Industry experts estimate that how much of every sales dollar is lost to employee and customer dishonesty?

   A. 1–2%
   B. 2–4%
   C. 4–6%
   D. 10%

   L.O. 15.1

3. Hospitality operators have difficulty maintaining storage facilities with adequate

   A. temperature.
   B. humidity.
   C. space.
   D. equipment.

   L.O. 15.2

4. What are the temperature requirements for nonhazardous food?

    A. Items must be stored at 40°F or below.
    B. Items must be stored at 140°F or above.
    C. Items must be stored at temperatures between 40°F and 140°F.
    D. There are no mandated temperature requirements.

    L.O. 15.2

5. What dictates who is allowed to enter the storage areas and who is allowed to obtain items from storage?

    A. Storeroom regulations
    B. Health codes
    C. Food and Drug Administration
    D. Storeroom employees

    L.O. 15.3

6. Although the storage areas of small operations are generally not managed systematically, what is the one exception?

    A. Sundries storeroom
    B. Liquor storeroom
    C. Meat storeroom
    D. Produce storeroom

    L.O. 15.3

7. If one unit of a restaurant chain needs frozen vegetables from another, the lending unit must complete which of the following?

    A. Stock requisition
    B. Physical inventory
    C. Transfer slip
    D. FSIS

    L.O. 15.3

8. A storeroom manager who has counted and valued all items in storage has conducted a(n)

    A. audit.
    B. inventory classification.
    C. perpetual inventory.
    D. physical inventory.

    L.O. 15.3

9. Which of the following can help small operators manage and control their storerooms?

    A. Using one-stop shopping
    B. Sending expensive items to the in-process inventory
    C. Owner/manager issuing par stocks of inexpensive items to users
    D. Stock clerk retrieving additional expensive items if they are needed during the shift

    L.O. 15.4

10. Comparing the number of expensive items used during a shift to what was sold is called

    A. inventory control and security.
    B. critical-item inventory analysis.
    C. skimming.
    D. theoretical inventory valuation.

    L.O. 15.4

88

CHAPTER 16

SECURITY IN THE PURCHASING FUNCTION

Learning Objectives

After reading this chapter, you should be able to:

16.1 Describe the security problems associated with the purchasing, receiving, storing, and issuing function.

16.2 Identify methods used to prevent security problems related to purchasing, receiving, storing, and issuing.

Chapter 16 Study Outline

1. Security problems include any of the following:

   - **Kickbacks** occur when a buyer, user-buyer, or receiver colludes with a supplier, salesperson, or delivery agent to conceal discrepancies between what an operation pays for and what it receives. Invariably, such collusion usually results in operation personnel receiving some money or goods, while supplier personnel increase their company's sales or profits.

   - **Invoice scams** occur when someone diverts a bill payment to a fictitious company or account.

   - **Supplier and receiver error** can result in potentially large losses if invoices containing arithmetic errors are not caught and corrected.

   - **Inventory theft** can be prevented easily by restricting access to all receiving and storage areas.

   - **Inventory padding**, in which the value of an ending inventory is inflated then covered up by removing an equal amount of merchandise from storage, is an illegal way for supervisors to decrease their cost-of-food-sold figure so as to earn a better performance bonus.

   - **Inventory substitutions** occur when employees switch high-quality goods for inferior ones, then consume or sell the goods on the black market.

   - **Telephone sales scams** and **unauthorized shipment scams** often result in operations paying for either inferior product or product never wanted in the first place.

- **Inability to segregate operating activities,** as is the case when a buyer does his or her own receiving, provides this employee with ample opportunities to cover up many dishonest behaviors.

- A wide range of **suspicious employee behavior** can tip off management that someone is planning to steal or pilfer.

2. To prevent security breaches, managers should:

   - Select honest suppliers.

   - Employ honest employees.

   - Design physical facilities so that tight, effective security conditions can be maintained.

3. Operators can take many specific steps to prevent theft and pilferage:

   - Document cash paid-outs carefully.

   - Question all invoices, especially those addressed to a post office box or an unfamiliar supplier.

   - Separate the purchasing and bill-paying functions.

   - Physically cancel paperwork on all completed transactions to avoid double-paying a bill.

   - Conduct random, unannounced independent audits.

   - Use a shopping service periodically to spot any illegal front-of-the-house activities.

   - While some operations use personality and drug tests to prescreen employee candidates, other operations avoid these tests due to potential testing error and privacy concerns.

   - Bond the operations against employee theft.

   - Use a trash compactor to eliminate "trash-can" pilfering.

   - Have employees leave through one door.

   - Prevent employees from parking near the building.

   - Locate employee locker rooms to discourage theft.

   - Do not allow delivery agents to loiter in unauthorized areas.

   - Do not rush receivers when they are checking in a delivery.

   - Keep all unauthorized people out of the back of the house.

   - Invest in cost-effective physical barriers such as time locks and other heavy-duty locks, good storeroom lighting, closed-circuit television, security guards, and a perimeter alarm system.

   - Eliminate other collusion opportunities by separating buying, receiving, storing, and issuing activities if possible.

   - Periodically check AP prices of current suppliers with other suppliers.

- Avoid hiring employees who have relatives working for a current supplier.
- If possible, remove items from shipping containers when storing, to minimize "inventory shrinkage."
- Avoid putting up cash deposits.
- If a supplier can be trusted, consider becoming a house account.
- Prevent unrecorded merchandise from getting into the storage facilities.
- Do not be rushed into purchasing inadequate products.
- Develop an approved supplier list to better control the possibility of kickbacks.
- Avoid purchasing merchandise in single-service packaging, as it is easy to pilfer.
- Restrict access to and maintain tight control of all high-cost products.
- If affordable, adopt computer technology that can calculate theoretical-inventory value.
- Only allow authorized personnel access to all records.

Chapter 16 Exercises

1. Identify each of the following as a kickback (K), invoice scam (IS), inventory padding (IP), or inventory substitution (SUB).

_____a. The ending inventory amount is increased so that management believes the supervisor has produced a highly favorable food cost.

_____b. A system in which a buyer colludes with a supplier, salesperson, or delivery person to receive inferior merchandise while paying for a superior product so that the buyer and accomplice(s) pocket the difference in price.

_____c. Half an order is delivered in the morning, while the other half promised in the afternoon never arrives; the bookkeeper overlooks the shortage.

_____d. A bill is sent to a fictitious company; the co-conspirators pocket the payment.

_____e. High-quality merchandise is removed from the storeroom and replaced with inferior goods.

L.O. 16.1

2. What is a toner-phoner?

_____

_____

_____

L.O. 16.1

3. Name two reasons why many hospitality operations do not use honesty testing to screen potential employees.

- _____

- _____

L.O. 16.2

4. Indicate whether each of the following statements is true (T) or false (F).

_____a. Buyers should never pay the bills.

_____b. Bonding provides information only about the future.

_____c. For security purposes, it is best for all employees to use one door.

_____d. Operators should compare what they are paying current suppliers with AP prices available from other suppliers for the same type of merchandise.

_____e. Everything should be left in shipping containers before being stored.

_____f. It is worthwhile to become a house account for one or more suppliers whose integrity you trust completely.

_____g. Access to all high-cost products should be restricted.

L.O. 16.2

Chapter 16 Check-in

1. According to U.S. Department of Commerce estimates, what fraction of employees steals from their companies at least once a year?
   A. 1/8
   B. 1/3
   C. 1/2
   D. 3/4
   L.O. 16.1

2. When a short order is delivered and the bookkeeper ignores the shortage, which security breach results?
   A. Invoice padding
   B. Fictitious invoice
   C. Kickback
   D. Bribery
   L.O. 16.1

3. An invoice scam results when
   A. the buyer agrees to pay a slightly higher AP price and receives an under-the-table payment from the supplier.
   B. a conspirator sends an invoice that has already been paid through to the bookkeeper, who pays it again.
   C. someone diverts a bill payment to a fictitious company or a fictitious account.
   D. items are weighed on inaccurate scales.
   L.O. 16.1

4. Hal increased the ending inventory amount from $20,000 to $22,000 so that managers thought that he had produced a highly favorable food cost for the month. What kind of security breach did Hal commit?

   A. Inventory substitution
   B. Inventory theft
   C. Inventory padding
   D. Inventory scamming

L.O. 16.1

5. In operations that are unable to segregate operating activities, the most common potential problem are buyers who

   A. pay for the products they order.
   B. issue the products they order.
   C. store the products they order.
   D. receive the products they order.

L.O. 16.1

6. Why do hospitality operators have trouble with pilferage?

   A. Products that hospitality operators use can easily be converted into cash.
   B. Hospitality operators tend to hire dishonest employees.
   C. Dishonest employees who are caught are seldom fired.
   D. Hospitality operators are reluctant to employ integrity tests.

L.O. 16.2

7. To reduce the possibility of double-paying an invoice,

   A. make some physical mark on it to indicate that payment has been made.
   B. file it quickly into a "paid" folder.
   C. call the supplier to minimize collusion.
   D. ask the receiver to look over the invoice one more time.

L.O. 16.2

8. If done on a random, unannounced basis, which of the following can help deter theft and pilferage?

   A. Drug tests
   B. Bonding
   C. Reference checks
   D. Audits

L.O. 16.2

9. If employee locker rooms cannot be located within a reasonable distance for spot checks, what can operators do to deter theft?

   A. Equip lockers with see-through screens instead of solid doors.
   B. Do surprise spot checks of the contents of lockers.
   C. Establish a surveillance camera in the locker room.
   D. Subject all suspect employees to polygraph tests.

L.O. 16.2

10. Operators should try not to hire employees who have

   A. disabilities.
   B. relatives working for suppliers.
   C. large families.
   D. worked for suppliers in the past.

L.O. 16.2

CHAPTER 17

FRESH PRODUCE

Learning Objectives

After reading this chapter, you should be able to:

17.1   Explain the selection factors for fresh produce, including government grades.

17.2   Describe the process of purchasing, receiving, storing, and issuing fresh produce.

Chapter 17 Study Outline

1. The purchasing of fresh produce requires a great deal of skill and knowledge.

    *   There are hundreds of varieties of fresh produce items and numerous supply sources.

    *   To make better produce-buying decisions, some buyers subscribe to trade publications that provide current information on produce prices and quality.

2. Fresh produce selection factors include:

    *   Intended use
    *   Exact name
    *   U.S. government inspection and grades (or equivalent)
    *   Packers' brands (or equivalent)
    *   Product size
    *   Size of container
    *   Type of packaging material
    *   Packaging procedure
    *   Minimum weight per case
    *   Product yield
    *   Point of origin
    *   Color
    *   Product form
    *   Degree of ripeness
    *   Ripening process used
    *   Preservation method
    *   Supplier dependability

3. When purchasing fresh produce:

    *   Obtain The Produce Marketing Association Fresh Produce Reference Manual for Food Service.

    *   Decide on the exact type of produce and the quality desired.

    *   Prepare a specification for each item.

    *   Consider all suppliers who are likely to satisfy the operation's needs, including local farmers or even a garden run by the operation itself.

4. To receive the correct amount of produce at the specified quality, receivers should:
   - Visually inspect the top layer of a carton, and then check the weight of the entire carton.
   - Randomly sample a proportion of containers, checking count, size, and quality throughout them.
   - Strive to develop a partner-like relationship with vendors.
5. Store fresh produce immediately at the proper temperature and humidity levels.
   - Since produce left at room temperature deteriorates very quickly, moving produce into a refrigerated area immediately is crucial.
   - While some types of produce are packaged to improve shelf life, others need to be repackaged.
   - Contrary to popular opinion, produce should not be washed before it is stored.
   - To extend shelf life, only handle produce when absolutely necessary.
6. Fresh produce often bypasses the central storage facility and goes directly to the food-production department.
   - To extract better value from higher-paid cooks and chefs, some operations issue fresh produce that's already been cleaned, chopped, peeled, or otherwise made ready-to-go.
   - Proper stock rotation of fresh produce is vital to minimize spoilage.

Chapter 17 Exercises

1. The following statements are false. Rewrite each so that it is true.
   a. When buying fresh produce, there tend to be few daily variations within the same product line.

   _____

   _____

   b. A single, year-round price for fresh produce is the norm.

   _____

   c. Keeping track of the types, varieties, and styles of fresh produce is a task often performed only by large hospitality operations.

   _____

   _____

   _____

   d. Packers' brands present no problems for buyers who use them.

   _____

e. A lug is a device used to weigh produce.

_____

f. Packaging generally has no effect on the AP price of produce.

_____

g. Slab-packed produce is layered neatly in the container.

_____

h. A decay allowance represents the amount discounted from each order of produce placed by a buyer.

_____

_____

i. Fresh produce is always ordered for full ripeness upon delivery.

_____

j. It is considered unethical for produce suppliers to wax fresh items.

_____

k. Local farmers are typically cheaper and offer more variety at lower prices than larger suppliers.

_____

_____

L.O. 17.1

2. Match the grading terms with its description.

_____(1) No. 1
_____(2) No. 3
_____(3) Field run
_____(4) Fancy
_____(5) Commercial
_____(6) Combination
_____(7) No. 2

a. Ungraded
b. Top-quality produce
c. Low quality—just barely acceptable for packing under normal packing conditions
d. Slightly less than U.S. No. 1
e. Bulk of products produced
f. Mixture of U.S. No. 1 and U.S. No. 2
g. Much less quality than U.S. No. 1, but very superior to U.S. No. 3

L.O. 17. 1

3. List the four steps required to purchase fresh product.

- _____

- _____

- _____

- _____

L.O. 17.2

4. Name at least three considerations that are crucial to proper storage of fresh produce.

- _____

- _____

- _____

L.O. 17.2

Chapter 17 Check-in

1. Who usually specifies the quality levels desired of fresh produce?

   A. Buyer
   B. Receiver
   C. Supplier
   D. Owner/manager

   L.O. 17.1

2. If Hank wants to purchase peaches to use in a fruit cup but wants to avoid paying a premium price for the appearance of the peaches, he must

   A. indicate the exact name of the product desired.
   B. specify the product size.
   C. request a particular packing procedure.
   D. exactly identify the performance requirement or intended use.

   L.O. 17.1

3. Currently, the USDA has grading standards for approximately how many types of fruits, vegetables, and nuts?

   A. 100
   B. 150
   C. 300
   D. 1,000

   L.O. 17.1

4. The grade that most retailers purchase is

   A. No. 1.
   B. fancy.
   C. commercial.
   D. No. 2.

   L.O. 17.1

5. A produce product that is randomly placed into a container with no added packaging is said to be

   A. layered.
   B. cell-packed.
   C. slab-packed.
   D. ready-to-serve.

   L.O. 17.1

6. When a buyer purchases an item in something other than its original form,

   A. the item is fully ripened and ready to serve.
   B. the buyer must indicate the desired preservation method.
   C. varying degrees of value have been added.
   D. the item tends to be less expensive than it would be in its original form.

   L.O. 17.1

7. Which of the following is not as prevalent in the fresh-produce trade as it is for processed food and nonfood items?

   A. House accounts
   B. Bid buying
   C. Pick-your-own establishments
   D. Organic products

   L.O. 17.2

8. Ideally, where should a receiver inspect deliveries of fresh produce?

   A. On the dock
   B. In refrigerated quarters
   C. On the delivery truck
   D. In the production department

   L.O. 17.2

9. Before being stored, produce items should not be

   A. washed.
   B. handled.
   C. exposed to air.
   D. exposed to light.

   L.O. 17.2

10. Since produce items tend to spoil quickly, buyers should

   A. have a great deal of experience handling these products.
   B. be extremely well paid.
   C. stay abreast of fluctuating prices throughout the year.
   D. purchase no more than necessary.

   L.O. 17.2

CHAPTER 18

Processed Produce and Other Grocery Items

Learning Objectives

After reading this chapter, you should be able to:

18.1   Identify management considerations surrounding the selection and procurement of processed produce and other grocery items.

18.2   Explain the selection factors for processed produce and other grocery items, including government grades.

18.3   Describe the process of purchasing, receiving, storing, and issuing processed produce and other grocery items.

Chapter 18 Study Outline

1.   Management must decide which products should be fresh and which should be processed.
   - Some cooking methods result in food that does not taste all that different than its processed counterpart.
   - Some processing methods, such a fresh-frozen goods, offer a means of extending the availability of perishable items, but processing's effect on taste and quality is critical.
   - While many processed food items were originally created to extend shelf life, once opened and heated these same products often have very short in-process shelf lives.
   - For any given product, there may be several methods of processing available, including canned, shelf-stable, frozen, pickled, fermented, dried, or dehydrated.
   - While determining the most profitable proportion of processed product to fresh product for a recipe is extremely time-consuming without computerized, management-information systems, calculating such substitutions offers great money-saving potential.

2.   Other considerations regarding purchasing processed food items include:
   - Taking too lax an attitude toward the purchasing, inventory, and issuing of items such as condiments, since only a small amount of the total purchase dollars are involved.
   - Purchasing one processed food often leads to the need to buy other products or equipment.

- Taking the time to analyze both the economic and substitution value of opportunity buys and long-term contracts properly.
- Deciding which container size to buy—weighing higher AP prices of smaller packages against additional labor needed to prepare bulk-sized goods.

3. The owner/manager should evaluate the following selection factors when purchasing processed produce and other grocery items:
   - Intended use
   - Exact name, including the federal government's "standards of identity" for over 235 processed items
   - U.S. government inspection and grades (or equivalent)
   - Packers' brands (or equivalent)
   - Product size, especially the **"count"** on the number of items inside a canned or packaged item (higher counts equal a larger number of small-sized items, while lower counts equal a lower number of large-sized items.)
   - Size of container
   - Type of packaging material
   - Packaging procedure
   - Drained weight (servable weight)
   - Type of processing
   - Color
   - Product form
   - Packing medium
   - Use of additives and preservatives
   - Information beyond what is federally required, including packing and freshness dates, serving cost data, lot numbers, and Child Nutrition (CN) labels
   - One-stop shopping opportunities
   - AP price
   - Supplier services: though they are usually nominal for canned products, buyers prefer suppliers who can give them reasonable **"break points"**—number of items they have to buy to receive a quantity discount.
   - Local supplier or national source

4. When purchasing processed produce and other grocery items, specs should be prepared after consulting reference materials, determining need, and deciding on daily or long-term delivery.
   - When using a long-term contract, a buyer or owner/manager should perform a **cutting test** on products, which involves keeping some of the original unopened packages to compare with product subsequently delivered.

5. To receive processed goods properly:
   - Check canned goods for swelling, leaks, rust, dents, or broken seals, as these all suggest contamination problems.
   - Check dried goods for condition of container and if product is visible, check for mold, broken pieces, or odd appearance.
   - Check frozen goods for any sign of thawing, refreezing, or freezer burn.
6. When storing processed produce and other grocery items, generally accepted procedures should be followed for canned and bottled products, dried items, and frozen products.

Chapter 18 Exercises

1. What is the overall advantage of processed food items over their fresh counterparts?

   _____

   _____

   _____

   L.O. 18.1

2. What must be done to dried food items before they can be used?

   _____

   _____

   _____

   L.O. 18.1

3. What are the four factors generally considered by U.S. government inspectors when grading canned items?
   - _____
   - _____
   - _____
   - _____

   L.O. 18.2

4. What does it mean if a processed item contains a "Grade A" seal but not a "U.S. Grade A" seal?

_____

_____

_____

L.O. 18.2

5. Alex, the new buyer for Spaghetti Café, must decide whether to start purchasing canned tomatoes rather than fresh tomatoes for all of the operation's sauces.

a. Indicate which selection factors Alex should consider and why consideration of each factor is important.

_____

_____

_____

_____

L.O. 18.2

b. What type of testing might Alex want to perform on the canned tomatoes?

_____

_____

L.O. 18.2, 18.3

c. What should Alex specifically check for immediately after opening the cans?

_____

_____

L.O. 18.3

d. If Alex opts to purchase large quantities of canned tomatoes, what should Spaghetti Café's receiving check when the shipments arrive?

_____

_____

L.O. 18.3

e. What should the operation's storeroom manager ensure when storing the products?

_____

_____

_____

L.O. 18.3

Chapter 18 Check-in

1. An operation's selection of a processing method is influenced by which of the following?

   A. Container size
   B. Product size
   C. Need for convenience
   D. EP price

   L.O. 18.1

2. What is an advantage of buying many dehydrated food items?

   A. No refrigeration is necessary.
   B. No reconstitution is necessary.
   C. They are packaged in a uniform manner.
   D. They are inexpensive.

   L.O. 18.1

3. Smaller packages of processed food and other grocery items have

   A. lower AP prices per unit than larger packages.
   B. higher AP prices per unit than larger packages.
   C. lower EP prices per unit than larger packages.
   D. higher EP prices per unit than larger packages.

   L.O. 18.1

4. Products packed under continuous inspection of the U.S. Department of Agriculture carry which of the following?

   A. U.S. No. 1
   B. U.S. government shield
   C. U.S. Grade A
   D. CN label

   L.O. 18.2

5. Companies that package the best quality merchandise, but will pack lower-quality products if these items carry some other brand name are referred to as

   A. generic brands.
   B. packers' brands.
   C. alternative brands.
   D. premium brands.

   L.O. 18.2

6. When purchasing canned products, which of the following should a buyer consider?

   A. Volume
   B. Size
   C. Area
   D. Weight

   L.O. 18.2

7. While supplier services may not be as crucial in the purchase of processed food, buyers do expect reasonable

   A. break points.
   B. cutting tests
   C. AP prices.
   D. EP portions.

   L.O. 18.2

8. As the typical hospitality operation grows, it shows fewer tendencies to use

   A. convenience food and other grocery items.
   B. detailed specifications for buying processed produce.
   C. one-stop shopping for processed produce.
   D. generic brands of processed produce.

   L.O. 18.2

9. A buyer who enters into a long-term contract on a bid basis will need

   A. dropped shipments.
   B. break points.
   C. detailed specifications.
   D. opportunity buys.

   L.O. 18.3

10. When storing dried products, which of the following should employees make sure is not present in the storeroom?

    A. Broken seals
    B. Dampness
    C. Freezer burn
    D. Container swelling

    L.O. 18.3

CHAPTER 19

Learning Objectives

After reading this chapter, you should be able to:

19.1   Explain the selection factors for dairy products, including government grades.

19.2   Describe the process of purchasing, receiving, storing, and issuing dairy products.

Chapter 19 Study Outline

1. The following are selection factors for purchasing dairy products:

    *   Intended use, including relative importance of factors such as flavor or appearance

    *   Exact name, often based on minimum or maximum amounts of butterfat

    *   While few dairy products are graded, buyers do consider U.S. government grades (or equivalent) for products such as milk, cheese, and butter.

    *   Ice cream has a non-government grading system based on amount of butterfat.

    *   Pull dates—the last date an item can be sold—are a common type of terminology.

    *   Packers' brands (or equivalent) are important, as remarkable taste differences can occur between manufacturers' cheeses, yogurts, ice cream, sherbet, and dry milk.

    *   Product size

    *   Size of container is important, especially considering the highly perishable nature of dairy products.

    *   Type of packaging material

    *   Packaging procedure can be important, especially for single-serve dairy products.

    *   Product yield

    *   Product form

    *   While refrigeration is the most common preservation method for dairy products, some products like are pasteurized at ultra high temperatures (UHT), and then aseptically packaged to increase shelf life dramatically.

    *   **Butterfat content**—in general, the greater the amount of butterfat, the higher the AP price.

- Milk solids' content must be indicated if buyers desire fewer solids than maximum allowed.
- **Overrun**—amount of air in a frozen dairy product
- Chemical additives
- Some buyers prefer cows' milk from herds that have not been given hormones such as bST, rBGH, or rBST.
- How the product is processed—some buyers prefer "natural" cheeses that have the absolute minimum of additives.
- **Nondairy products** often have a lower AP price, but nutritionists and customers alike question their nutritional merit, and these products often do not substitute well in recipes calling for dairy products.
- AP price
- One-stop shopping

2. When purchasing dairy products, a buyer must first determine what is needed, and then decide on the most appropriate delivery schedule.
   - In general, a daily dairy schedule is preferred for buyers to ensure quality.
   - Recipes calling for milk can often use a dry milk substitute to reduce overall EP cost without diminishing quality.

3. Since most dairy items are perishable, receivers should consider moving a delivery into the refrigerated area for inspection.
   - Since many dairy products are delivered on a standing-order basis, receivers need to make sure the items delivered reflect the items invoiced.

4. Proper dairy product storage procedures include:
   - Keep items refrigerated until needed in production.
   - If possible, use a separate dairy refrigerator to avoid flavor contamination from other products.
   - All items should be rotated on the shelves properly.

5. Proper issuing procedures for dairy products should include:
   - Making sure only the day's amount of dairy products is issued to reduce spoilage
   - Creating sound, in-process inventory and supervision practices to reduce spoilage and pilferage

Chapter 19 Exercises

1. Indicate whether each of the following statements is true (T) or false (F).

_____a. A majority of dairy products carry a standard of identity set by the federal government.

_____b. Milk is a good medium for harmful bacteria.

_____c. Ice cream in which eggs have been used as a thickening agent might be called "premium."

_____d. The difference in taste between one supplier and another can be remarkable for dry milk.

_____e. Packaging materials for dairy products are standardized throughout the industry.

_____f. Pasteurization using ultra high temperatures yields a dairy product with a taste similar to fresh, refrigerated, whole, fluid milk.

_____g. The federal government mandates the minimum amount of nonfat, dried milk solids that some dairy products can have.

_____h. In a controlled state, the buyer must pay at least the minimum AP price.

L.O. 19.1

2. What role does butterfat content play in the purchasing of dairy products?

_____

_____

_____

L.O. 19.1

3. What is overrun? What effect does it have on a dairy product?

_____

_____

_____

L.O. 19.1

4. Why do many operators use nondairy items?

_____

_____

_____

L.O. 19.1

5. Complete each sentence below.

   a. Preparing elaborate specifications for dairy products is usually unnecessary unless

   _____

   b. It is best to avoid doing business with independent farmers because

   _____

   c. It can sometimes be difficult to check that all dairy items ordered have been received because

   _____

   d. As much as possible, dairy items should be stored

   _____

L.O. 19.2

Chapter 19 Check-in

1. Which component of dairy products has a direct correlation with AP price?

   A. Milk solids
   B. Flavoring
   C. Syrup
   D. Butterfat

   L.O. 19.1

2. Which dairy product is typically graded?

   A. Ice cream
   B. Cheese
   C. Milk
   D. Yogurt

   L.O. 19.1

3. Fluid milk grades are based primarily on the finished product's

   A. standard of identity.
   B. bacterial count.
   C. product yield.
   D. intended use.

   L.O. 19.1

4. Heating milk to kill pathogens is a process known as

   A. homogenization.
   B. pasteurization.
   C. preservation.
   D. fortification.

   L.O. 19.1

5. Most dairy items must be

   A. refrigerated.
   B. frozen.
   C. canned.
   D. left at room temperature.

   L.O. 19.1

6. The amount of air in a frozen dairy product is referred to as

   A. volume.
   B. emulsification.
   C. overrun.
   D. fluff.

   L.O. 19.1

7. Dairies often treat their herds with synthetic hormones designed to

   A. diversify milk variety.
   B. increase milk production.
   C. enhance milk flavor.
   D. produce low-fat milk.

   L.O. 19.1

8. What type of dairy-product delivery schedule is preferred in the hospitality industry?

   A. Hourly
   B. Daily
   C. Weekly
   D. Monthly

   L.O. 19.2

9. Which dairy item is typically delivered on a standing-order basis?

   A. Milk
   B. Cheese
   C. Ice cream
   D. Butter

   L.O. 19.2

10. Maintaining a separate dairy refrigerator is recommended because dairy products

   A. are very expensive.
   B. have a short shelf life.
   C. can easily pick up odors.
   D. must be kept colder than other types of refrigerated food.

   L.O. 19.2

CHAPTER 20

EGGS

Learning Objectives

After reading this chapter, you should be able to:

20.1   Explain the selection factors for eggs, including government grades.

20.2   Describe the process of purchasing, receiving, storing, and issuing eggs.

Chapter 20 Study Outline

1.   Selection factors for purchasing eggs include:

   - Intended use, including the relative importance of flavor and appearance

   - Exact name—generally, names cause little difficulty in selecting eggs.

   - U.S. government inspection and grades (or equivalent) are quite familiar for fresh shell eggs, with most buyers opting for Grade A eggs with a rating of high, medium, or low.

   - Packers' brands (or equivalent) for fresh shell eggs are generally not an important factor for most hospitality operations.

   - Product size

   - Size of container

   - Type of packaging material—while fresh-egg packaging is standardized and not much of concern to buyers, processed-egg products vary considerably, and care should be taken to prevent spoilage.

   - Packaging procedure

   - Color—in some areas, customers prefer brown eggs, although there is no flavor or nutritional differences.

   - Product form

   - Preservation methods for fresh eggs include such techniques as refrigeration, oil spraying (dipping), overwrapping, and controlled-atmosphere storage.

   - Supplier trustworthiness

2. Buyers usually choose an egg supplier based on who can provide the freshest product.
   - Independent farmers often get shell eggs to operations quickly and allow buyers to bargain for AP prices; buyers should still be cautious, however, since government inspectors may not have checked the products of these farmers.
3. When receiving eggs, check them for cracks, dirt, and lack of uniformity. Ensure that the temperature meets your refrigeration requirements.
   - The American Egg Board recommends randomly breaking a few eggs from a new delivery to ensure the product is fresh.
4. As with dairy products, eggs should be kept in refrigerated storage, be separated from odorous foods such as onions or cabbage, and be issued only as needed.

Chapter 20 Exercises

1. What will a buyer receive if he/she orders each of the following?
   a. Storage eggs

   _____

   b. Fresh shell eggs

   _____

   c. Egg products

   _____

   d. Eggs

   _____

L.O. 20.1

2. Describe the characteristics of each of the following egg quality grades.
   - AA

   _____

   _____

   - A

   _____

   _____

   - B

   _____

   _____

L.O. 20.1

3. Place the following egg sizes in order from smallest (1) to largest (6).

_____a. Extra large

_____b. Small

_____c. Peewee

_____d. Jumbo

_____e. Large

_____f. Medium

L.O. 20.1

4. What form of eggs is available in shrink-wrapped packaging?

_____

_____

L.O. 20.1

5. Place the following preservation methods in order from most effective (1) to least effective (4) in preserving eggs.

_____Oil dipping

_____Refrigeration

_____Overwrapping

_____Oil spraying

L.O. 20.2

6. Name three potential disadvantages to buying fresh eggs from independent farmers.

• _____

• _____

• _____

L.O. 20.2

7. List at least three characteristics to check when receiving eggs in any form.

• _____

• _____

• _____

L.O. 20.2

Chapter 20 Check-in

1. A buyer who orders "fresh shell eggs" will receive which of the following?

    A. Shell eggs older than four weeks
    B. Shell eggs less than four weeks old
    C. Eggs that have been removed from their shells
    D. An egg product in liquid, frozen, or dried form

    L.O. 20.1

2. Facilities that process eggs and, thus, break their shells are called

    A. hen houses.
    B. breaker plants.
    C. Cryovac facilities.
    D. egg factories.

    L.O. 20.1

3. How many possible government grades are there for eggs?

    A. Three
    B. Five
    C. Six
    D. Nine

    L.O. 20.1

4. Buyers should insist on continuous government inspection of shell eggs because

    A. fresh shell eggs are graded primarily on interior quality factors, which are difficult for an unskilled buyer to assess.
    B. government inspectors employ devices and processes unavailable to most hospitality buyers.
    C. eggs are potentially hazardous food.
    D. the AA grade is difficult to obtain.

    L.O. 20.1

5. What is the most common quality indicator for fresh shell eggs?

    A. Packers' brand
    B. Packaging procedure
    C. Preservation method
    D. Federal grade

    L.O. 20.1

6. Eggs purchased to be fried, scrambled, poached, or prepared in omelets are usually which size?

    A. Large
    B. Jumbo
    C. Peewee
    D. Medium

    L.O. 20.1

7. The breed of the hen determines which of the following?

    A. Size of the egg
    B. Consistency of the yolk
    C. Color of the egg
    D. Shelf life of the egg

    L.O. 20.1

8. What is the most common preservation for fresh shell eggs?

    A. Oil spraying
    B. Refrigeration
    C. Overwrapping
    D. Controlled-atmosphere storage

    L.O. 20.2

9. What is one potential advantage of buying shell eggs from independent farmers?
    A. Government inspectors check the eggs of these farmers.
    B. Their hens are well managed.
    C. They may be able to deliver shell eggs to buyers one or two days after laying.
    D. Their flocks are the ideal age for egg laying.
L.O. 20.2

10. Which of the following should alert the receiver that frozen egg products have been refrozen?
    A. Crystallization
    B. Foul odor
    C. Lack of uniformity
    D. Staining
L.O. 20.2

CHAPTER 21

POULTRY

Learning Objectives

After reading this chapter, you should be able to:

21.1   Explain the selection factors for poultry, including government grades.

21.2   Describe the process of purchasing, receiving, storing, and issuing poultry.

Chapter 21 Study Outline

1. Selection factors for purchasing poultry include:

    *   Intended use—buyers often buy fresh poultry with several different dishes in mind; they also tend to examine substitutions more carefully than they do with other products.

    *   Exact name—federal standards of identity for fresh poultry consider birds' age at time of slaughter and birds' sex, while other terminology such as **"free-range"** or **"Kosher"** refer to specific growing/slaughtering methods.

    *   U.S. government grades (or equivalent) consider the birds' conformation, fleshing, fat covering, and other factors such as bruises, excessive pinfeathers, broken bones, or missing parts.

    *   Grades range from Grade A—a full-fleshed bird that is well finished and has an attractive appearance, to Grade C—a less-attractive bird with dressing defects and possibly missing some of its parts.

    *   Packers' brands (or equivalent) are not as important for buyers purchasing fresh or fresh-frozen poultry, although some loyalty does seem to exist for raw turkey or duck.

    *   Product size for raw poultry products is expressed in terms of acceptable weight ranges; in general, the larger the bird, the higher its yield.

    *   Product yield with processed poultry is often expressed in terms of maximum yield, or minimum trim expected.

    *   Size of container

    *   Type of packaging material varies greatly, even among fresh poultry, and buyers should reject any packaging that might reduce the product's shelf life.

- "**Ice pack procedure**" is a common packaging procedure for fresh birds, in which the birds are slab-packed with crushed ice on top of them. Other procedures include cello packs, gas-flushed packs, marinade packs, and individually quick frozen (IQF).
- Product form varies considerably, from whole birds with or without organ meats to birds cut into a specific number of pieces.
- Preservation method is generally either refrigerated or frozen.
- Differences in AP prices for raw poultry are generally the result of travel costs, while AP prices on processed poultry can vary considerably.
- Supplier trustworthiness is, as always, a major concern.

2. Most foodservice buyers purchase U.S. Grade A quality; however, Grade B can be used when appearance is not important.

3. Proper receiving techniques for poultry include:
   - Inspecting items in a refrigerated area if possible
   - Checking to make sure boxes have not been repacked, and that quality corresponds to the grade shield on the box
   - Weighing several birds to ensure they are within the specified weight range
   - Streamlining procedures by using the **USDA's Acceptance Service**

4. Fresh poultry should be stored at the proper temperature and humidity for its form.
   - While the shelf life of fresh poultry can be extended up to a week by ensuring that it stays on ice, it is equally important that melted ice water runs out of the storage package.
   - Poultry should be handled as little as possible prior to production.

5. Proper stock rotation should be followed when issuing poultry.
   - Operators need to determine if poultry should be issued as is or ready-to-go (the item can be heated directly without additional prep).

Chapter 21 Exercises

1. Match each term on the left with its description on the right.

_____(1) Poultry

_____(2) 9- to 12-week-old chicken

_____(3) Capon

_____(4) Roaster

_____(5) Stewing hen

_____(6) Free-range

_____(7) Kosher

_____(8) Fleshing

_____(9) Grade A

_____(10) Procurement grades

_____(11) Soft-scald procedure

_____(12) Chill pack

_____(13) Freezer burn

_____(14) USDA Acceptance Service

a. Method of removing a bird's feathers to keep the bird tender

b. System of raising poultry so they are allowed to roam free during their lives

c. Broiler/fryer

d. Method that will help a buyer streamline the receiving process

e. Grading term referring to a bird's flesh development

f. 3- to 5-month-old chicken

g. Blanket term for all domesticated birds used for food

h. Highest grade given to poultry

i. Five- to eight-month-old chicken

j. Process of raising poultry according to Jewish dietary laws in which birds are kept free of hormones and chemicals

k. Result of refreezing or improperly freezing poultry

l. Chicken older than ten months

m. Grades given to poultry for use by institutional food services

n. Method of preserving poultry just short of freezing it

L.O. 21.1

2. Name three factors used by federal inspectors to grade poultry.

- _____

- _____

- _____

L.O. 21.1

3. Which process removes almost all traces of harmful bacteria in meats and fish and spoilage bacteria in fresh produce?

_____

L.O. 21.2

4. List three factors that a buyer should consider when evaluating potential poultry suppliers.

- _____

- _____

- _____

L.O. 21.2

5. How can the receiver check the quantity of poultry when it comes packed in ice?

_____

_____

_____

L.O. 21.2

Chapter 21 Check-in

1. If an operator cooks poultry with dry heat and wants a tender product, what kind of poultry should be purchased?

   A. Young bird
   B. Older bird
   C. Female bird
   D. Male bird

   L.O. 21.1

2. All raw poultry sold in interstate commerce and processed products must be

   A. fleshed.
   B. chill-packed.
   C. federally inspected.
   D. flushed.

   L.O. 21.1

3. Which of the following factors are considered by federal inspectors during grading?

   A. Age
   B. Gender
   C. Packaging
   D. Conformation

   L.O. 21.1

4. Which grade of poultry do buyers purchase when appearance is very important?

   A. U.S. Grade AA
   B. U.S. Grade A
   C. U.S. Grade B
   D. U.S. Grade C

   L.O. 21.1

5. Turkeys over twenty pounds will usually have
   A. more feathers than those under twenty pounds.
   B. more flavor than those under twenty pounds.
   C. more fat than those under twenty pounds.
   D. None of the above
   L.O. 21.1

6. Poultry placed in plastic bags with the air replaced by carbon dioxide come in
   A. marinade packs.
   B. carbon packs.
   C. cello packs.
   D. gas-flushed packs.
   L.O. 21.1

7. Both chill packs and ice packs are used to maintain temperatures of about
   A. 28°F to 29°F.
   B. 32°F.
   C. 35°F to 37°F.
   D. 45°F.
   L.O. 21.1

8. How long does it take to bring a frying chicken from birth to the dining room table?
   A. A few days
   B. A few weeks
   C. A few months
   D. One year
   L.O. 21.1

9. What is one thing that a receiver should check to determine the age of poultry?
   A. Color
   B. Product yield
   C. Amount of abdominal fat
   D. Government grade
   L.O. 21.2

10. If chickens are received in an ice pack, they should be stored so that melted ice
    A. refreezes.
    B. soaks into the birds.
    C. runs from the storage package.
    D. is ultimately consumed by patrons.
    L.O. 21.2

CHAPTER 22

FISH

Learning Objectives

After reading this chapter, you should be able to:

22.1   Explain the selection factors for fish, including government grades.

22.2   Describe the process of purchasing, receiving, storing, and issuing fish.

Chapter 22 Study Outline

1. Buying fresh fish can be one of the most complex and frustrating aspects of the purchasing function.

    *   Processed fish is easier to buy than fresh fish because there are relatively few suppliers of fresh fish.

    *   Farm-raised fish can reduce many of the risks of fresh-fish purchasing by ensuring stable quality and consistent supply.

2. Selection factors for purchasing fish include:

    *   Intended use

    *   Exact name—unfortunately, the fish industry routinely renames fish, often in an attempt to make an unappealing name more attractive.

    *   U.S. government grades (or equivalent) are provided, but few fish items are graded; the exception is a handful of processed fish products that are subject to standards of identity regulations (e.g., battered shrimp).

    *   While the **Packed Under Federal Inspection (PUFI)** seal indicates that the product is clean, safe, wholesome, and has been produced in a sanitary establishment, it is a voluntary program that many producers find too time-consuming to use. As a result, specifying PUFI for fish will significantly reduce the number of suppliers available to the operator.

    *   Packers' brands (or equivalent) are generally not a useful criterion for fish purchases.

    *   Product size varies depending on the type of fish or shellfish.

    *   Product yield

    *   Container size, type of packaging material, and packaging procedures for fish products have many similarities with those used in the poultry industry.

- Product form can include numerous types of convenience food made from processed fish, but buyers should always ensure that the culinary quality of such products is acceptable.
- Preservation methods can include frozen, dried, smoked, refrigerated, ice-packed, cello-packed, chill-packed, live-in-shell, and canned.
- Packing medium can affect the taste of fish products, such as tuna packed in oil or water.
- Point of origin can greatly influence the flavor of fish/shellfish.
- Supplier trustworthiness is absolutely crucial, given the variable availability, perishability, and high transport costs of fish.

3. When purchasing fish:
   - Acquire some reference materials about purchasing fish.
   - Locate a list of suppliers who operate in the buyer's local market.
   - Since fish availability is often sporadic, some buyers prepare a **statement of quality** for suppliers rather than traditional specifications.
   - The relationship between AP prices and quality with processed fish is more variable than with other product categories.
   - Before buyers choose fish on a supplier's "move list," they should consider whether their staff has the expertise and equipment to make the item properly, as well as whether to treat the product as a loss leader on their menu.

4. When receiving fish/shellfish:
   - Refrigerate all items immediately, weighing items with a scale located inside the refrigerator if possible.
   - Check that the fish has a mild scent that is not overly fishy; its flesh should be firm and spring back when pressed; gills should be bright pink or red, and if the head is still attached, eyes should be clear and bright.
   - Live items should be active.
   - Live-in-shell fish should be closed or close when touched.

5. To properly store fish/shellfish:
   - Refrigerate fresh fish and fresh, shucked shellfish at 32°F with no less than sixty-five percent relative humidity.
   - Store frozen fish at 0°F and canned fish at 50°F.
   - Live-in-shell fish such as lobster can be stored in water tanks or kept in original containers while covered with damp cloths.

6. Although most fresh fish go directly into production, proper stock rotation and strict control of the amount issued for any given shift are vital controls against excessive spoilage.

Chapter 22 Exercises

1. Why can buying fresh fish be a frustrating task?

   _____

   _____

   _____

L.O. 22.1

2. Even if buyers indicate the exact name of the items they want, why might they still receive unwanted items?

   _____

   _____

   _____

L.O. 22.1

3. How can buyers be sure that the fish products they purchase are safe, clean, and wholesome?

   _____

   _____

   _____

L.O. 22.1

4. Use a check mark to indicate which of the following statements are true.

   _____a.   A buyer who specifies that all her fish carry a PUFI seal would likely decrease the number of available suppliers.

   _____b.   The diseases afflicting fish supposedly do not threaten the people who eat them.

   _____c.   Continuous fish inspection is a voluntary program.

   _____d.   Packers' brands for fresh fish abound.

   _____e.   When purchasing whole fish products, a buyer can usually indicate the exact desired weight per item.

   _____f.   Live-in-shell fish items are usually packed in crush ice.

   _____g.   The packing medium used will significantly affect a fish product's culinary quality.

   _____h.   If a menu includes Lake Superior whitefish, the operation is not legally bound to serve whitefish from Lake Superior.

L.O. 22.1

5. Why is it especially important to trust the supplier when purchasing fresh fish?

_____

_____

_____

L.O. 22.1

6. What four things should a buyer consider before purchasing seafood bargains?

- _____

- _____

- _____

- _____

L.O.22.2

7. What are some of the difficulties associated with receiving fish?

_____

_____

_____

L.O. 22.2

Chapter 22 Check-in

1. Large restaurants that "grow their own" fresh fish engage in a practice called

    A. surimi.
    B. shucking.
    C. cultivation.
    D. aquaculture.

    L.O. 22.1

2. Even if a buyer indicates the exact name of a fish product, he or she might receive an unwanted item because

    A. the fish industry commonly renames fish.
    B. market terminology is constantly changing.
    C. federal standards of identity do not exist for fish.
    D. customers do not tend to accept exotic species.

    L.O. 22.1

3. A fish product suitable only for finished menu items would receive which of the following federal grades?

A. AA
B. A
C. B
D. C

L.O. 22.1

4. What fraction of fish consumed in the U.S. comes from other countries?

A. 1/3
B. 2/3
C. 3/4
D. 7/8

L.O. 22.1

5. Which of the following is not a useful selection factor for fresh fish items?

A. Packers' brands
B. Product size
C. Product yield
D. Size of container

L.O. 22.1

6. Fresh fish is often delivered in

A. moisture-proof, vapor-proof materials designed to withstand freezer temperatures.
B. fresh water.
C. cans.
D. reusable plastic tubs.

L.O. 22.1

7. What is a major issue that needs to be resolved when contemplating the purchase of processed fish products?

A. Packing medium
B. Product form
C. Substitution possibilities
D. Preservation method

L.O. 22.1

8. After acquiring some reference materials about purchasing fish, what should the buyer do?

A. Prepare detailed specifications for processed fish.
B. Decide on a supplier.
C. Obtain a list of approved, interstate fish suppliers operating in the area.
D. Determine the exact type of product and quality desired.

L.O. 22.2

9. When examining live fish, a receiver should ensure that the product is

A. thawed.
B. "slacked out."
C. very active.
D. lightweight for its size.

L.O. 22.2

10. Canned or bottled fish products should be stored

A. in a dry place.
B. on a bed of crushed ice.
C. in water tanks.
D. at 0°F.

L.O. 22.2

CHAPTER 23

MEAT

Learning Objectives

After reading this chapter, you should be able to:

23.1   Identify management considerations surrounding the selection and procurement

of meat.

23.2   Explain the selection factors for meat, including government grades.

23.3   Describe the process of purchasing, receiving, storing, and issuing meat.

Chapter 23 Study Outline

1. Beef, veal, pork, lamb, and processed meats are generally the types of meat products used in foodservice operations.

2. Management must make the following decisions with respect to meat:
   - Whether to offer meat on the menu, and if so, how tied to meat the menu should be
   - Whether there are alternatives for conventional meat items that might be more affordable and appropriate
   - Whether the quality desired can be consistently delivered by a supplier
   - What amount of in-house meat processing (if any) will be the most efficient and economical
   - Which strategies can best reduce the AP price while keeping the EP cost, profit margins, and dollar profits acceptable

3. Selection factors for purchasing meat include:
   - Intended use—consideration should be given both to a product's primary use and its secondary possibilities (e.g., leftovers).
   - Exact name—in addition to being knowledgeable about the various trade terms related to meat, buyers should use the **Institutional Meat Purchase Specifications (IMPS)** numbering system to order and receive the exact cut of meat desired.
   - U.S. government inspection. The USDA's Food Safety and Inspection Service (FSIS) uses a HACCP system at meat-slaughtering and meat-processing facilities to ensure food safety. Meat that passes this rigorous inspection is marked with a federal-inspection stamp.

- Voluntary grading programs are used to grade approximately fifty percent of the meat sold in the U.S. Beef grading has limiting rules based on maturity of the animal, with Class A designation given to animals nine to thirty months old at time of slaughter, Class B for animals from thirty to forty-two months, and Classes C,D, and E to animals over forty-two months. No Class C, D, or E animal can subsequently be labeled as "prime."

- Beef is evaluated for its "finish" (fatness), firmness of muscling, age and sex of animal, color of flesh, amount of external finish, carcass shape and form, and the number of defects and blemishes. The grades for beef are prime, choice, select, standard, commercial, and utility, cutter, and canner.

- The grades for lamb are prime, choice, good, and utility.

- The grades for pork, which are based almost exclusively on yield, are No.1, No.2, No.3, No. 4, and utility.

- The grades for veal are prime, choice, good, standard, utility, and cull.

- Product yield for beef and lamb is based on a voluntary grading service, with yield grades numbered one through five, with one being the highest yield.

- Packers' brands (or equivalent) allow meat producers to grade their own brands of meat or to highlight distinctive qualities of their meat (e.g., "certified organic" products).

- Product size—the IMPS stipulates the amount of accuracy needed based on the overall size of the final product.

- Container size is largely standardized in the meat channel of distribution.

- The type of packaging material is crucial to maintaining product quality and should be specified by buyers.

- Packaging procedures vary among suppliers, who are generally willing to accommodate buyers' needs if they are willing to pay for these services.

- While product form has been standardized through IMPS numbers, many products still are not noted in the *Meat Buyers Guide.* Buyers of these products often rely on packers' brand names to get what they want.

- Preservation methods include refrigerated, frozen, canned, dehydrated, pickled, curing, and smoking.

- A tenderization procedure such as **"dry aging"** adds to the AP price because it reduces the weight of the carcass and requires additional facilities and inventories. Buyers should never assume meat has been aged unless they specify it. Other tenderization procedures include spraying beef with mold, "wet aging" or "cryovac aging," electrification, adding enzyme to the meat, and mechanical methods such as "needling."

- Point of origin is often used to advertise an entrée, but buyers need to make sure their products actually come from that origin or risk breaking truth-in-menu laws.

- Some buyers seek out additional inspections by private inspectors to ensure that their meat products meet their standards.
- Imitation, low-fat meat products are becoming more popular, due to their lower AP prices and their potential health implications.
- One-stop shopping opportunities are not the rule in meat buying unless the shopping list contains only common items.
- AP price can be kept down by bid buying among acceptable suppliers.

4. To purchase meats, buyers should:
    - Get a copy of the *Meat Buyers Guide.*
    - Determine the operation's meat needs.
    - Prepare specifications for meats.
    - Evaluate suppliers.
    - Before buying meat, evaluate substitution possibilities.

5. Proper receiving techniques for meats include:
    - Inspecting deliveries in a refrigerated area
    - Having the chef or someone else who is knowledgeable about meat check the goods for quality
    - Rejecting meat with a bad odor or a slimy appearance
    - Insisting on proper packaging
    - Checking that the items are at their appropriate temperatures
    - Reviewing the quantities and prices carefully
    - Using the USDA's Acceptance Service or Product Examination Service if deemed necessary

6. The greatest challenge in storing meat is keeping the storage areas—and thus the products—clean and sanitary.
    - Fresh meat should be stored in either a separate meat refrigerator or a segregated area of the main refrigerator at 35°F to 40°F
    - Place cooked items above raw meats.

7. There is usually more control at the requisition stage when issuing meat than when issuing other food items.

Chapter 23 Exercises

Sean is the buyer-manager of Beef Eater, a new steak and chop restaurant scheduled to open next month in a Midwestern city.

1. What are some of the major managerial purchasing decisions he faces?

_____

_____

_____

L.O. 23.1

2. What type of meat is Sean likely to order in processed form?

_____

_____

L.O. 23.1

3. Sean has decided to purchase only the best beef product available. What federal quality grade will he purchase?

_____

L.O. 23.2

4. If Sean decides to purchase large cuts of meat for in-house fabrication, what four problems is he likely to face?

- _____

- _____

- _____

- _____

L.O. 23.2

5. List some of the ways that Sean might reduce his meat costs.

_____

_____

_____

L.O. 23.2

6. Sean is preparing specs for beef to be used in the operation's Beef Wellington entrée. Create this spec for Sean on a separate sheet of paper. Be sure to specify the intended use, exact name, grade, product yield, product size, packaging material, and desired AP price.

L.O. 23.3

Chapter 23 Check-in

1. Given the high cost of meats, an operation's goal is to
   A. utilize every edible morsel.
   B. find appropriate alternatives to conventional meat items.
   C. experiment with different grades of meat.
   D. determine which supplier offers the lowest AP price.

L.O. 23.1

2. Some foodservice operations perform a lot of in-house fabrication because it
   A. decreases the level of pilferage.
   B. provides better control of quality.
   C. requires fewer skilled laborers.
   D. reduces waste.

L.O. 23.1

3. Shrinking portion sizes, adding soybean extenders, and using a hedging procedure are all ways to
   A. add flavor to meat products.
   B. prevent contamination.
   C. reduce AP price.
   D. preserve meat products.

L.O. 23.1

4. To order and receive the exact cut of meat desired, meat buyers often refer to the _____ numbering system.
   A. suppliers'
   B. *Meat Buyers Monthly* magazine
   C. Institutional Meat Purchase Specifications
   D. Green Sheets

L.O. 23.2

5. Which of the following ensures that food safety conditions exist at all critical stages of foodhandling by reducing and eliminating defects that pass through traditional inspection?
   A. 1967 Wholesome Meat Act
   B. HACCP
   C. Department of Agriculture
   D. Federal Meat Inspection Act

L.O. 23.2

6. Cattle over forty-two months of age cannot receive which of the following grades?
   A. Select
   B. Choice
   C. Standard
   D. Prime

L.O. 23.2

7. Which of the following packaging is typically used for meat?

   A. Moisture-vapor proof materials
   B. Large, resealable cans
   C. Foil trays
   D. Shingle packs

L.O. 23.2

8. Which preservation method is used when meat is subjected to a combination of salt, sugar, sodium nitrite, and other ingredients?

   A. Curing
   B. Smoking
   C. Aging
   D. Chemical tenderizing

L.O. 23.2

9. Who should handle the quality check when meat is received?

   A. Owner/manager
   B. Receiving employee
   C. Chef
   D. Bookkeeper

L.O. 23.3

10. An employee typically needs which of the following to get meat from storage?

   A. The Meat Buyers Guide
   B. Stock requisition
   C. Management's permission
   D. Appropriate NAMP number

L.O. 23.3

CHAPTER 24

Learning Objectives

After reading this chapter, you should be able to:

24.1   Identify management considerations surrounding the selection and procurement of beverage alcohol and nonalcoholic beverages.

24.2   Explain the selection factors for beverage alcohol and nonalcoholic beverages.

24.3   Describe the process of purchasing, receiving, storing, and issuing beverage alcohol and nonalcoholic beverages.

Chapter 24 Study Outline

1. States' governments either directly **control** the sales, transport, and delivery of beverage alcohols or issue **licenses** for distributors to do so.

    *   Buyers in control states must follow the states' specific ordering and bill-paying procedures; this regulation often results in higher EP costs for beverage alcohol.

    *   While distributors in license states can often deliver products and offer credit terms, they still are restricted in the wholesale price they can charge and the amount and types of supplier services they can provide.

    *   Many beverage-alcohol companies provide exclusive distribution rights to one supplier in an area.

    *   Regardless of a state's regulatory situation, the relatively limited number of suppliers and the standardized nature of beverage alcohols make them one of the easiest items for a buyer to purchase.

2. Management must decide if the operation will offer alcohol; what quality of liquor to serve; if draft beer, bottled beer, or both should be sold; which wines should be sold; how many brands of distilled spirits and beer should be carried; and the appropriate menu prices for alcoholic beverages.

3. Selection factors for purchasing alcohol include:

    *   Intended use—wines may be packaged differently depending on whether they will be sold as house wine or by the bottle.

    *   Exact name

- Brand names (or equivalent) are the most fundamental selection factor with beverage alcohols.
- **Vintage**—the date a beverage was bottled—is an essential criterion of wines, some low-alcohol or lightly hopped beers, and other beverage alcohols with a limited shelf life.
- **Alcohol content** ranges from 3.2% to 6% for beer, 12% to 20% for wines, and 70-proof to 151-proof (35% to 75.5%) for distilled spirits.
- Container size is largely standardized for beverage alcohols, but buyers should select containers that best meet the operation's needs and the customers' preferences.
- Container type is also largely standardized, although there are some variations in how house wines can be purchased (e.g., bag-in-the-box or screw-top lids).
- Point of origin is an important selection factor for wines.
- Preservation method—while beer and wine need to be kept in cool, dark areas or under constant refrigeration (for draft beer), distilled spirits can be kept at room temperature.
- While AP prices often can be lowered though quantity buys and "post-off" discounts, import duties—taxes and tariffs levied on imported products—can have a major impact on AP prices.
- Supplier services for beverage alcohol include providing paperwork forms or online ordering services, offering local liquor code trainings, assisting in the creation of a wine list, and offering reasonable minimum-order requirements.

4. The biggest decision faced by buyers is the quantity of alcohol to order, especially when par-stock is well below minimum-order requirements.
   - Many distributors allow buyers to "break" a case; they may even allow buyers to combine several different items and receive a case price.

5. Much care goes into receiving alcohol because it is expensive and prone to theft.
   - Receivers need to check labels very carefully.
   - Kegs of beer require refrigeration, need to be handled carefully to avoid deteriorating quality, and carry deposits on them that need to be credited back to the operation.

6. Storage procedures for beverage alcohol include the following:
   - Keep separate, highly secure storage facilities for beverage alcohols.
   - Maintain a perpetual inventory for most beverage alcohols.
   - Store distilled spirits in well-sealed bottles at room temperature.
   - Store bottled wine on its side in a cool, dark area.
   - Refrigerate keg beer at 36°F to 38°F, making sure kegs rotate at least once every two weeks.
   - Bottled beer has a longer shelf life than kegs, but still should be kept in a cool, dark space.

7. Issuing beverage alcohol calls for strict scrutiny of owners and managers.

   - Perpetual inventories, secure storage facilities, careful control of stock requisitions, and keen oversight of the bar are all norms when it comes to beverage alcohols.

8. Purchasing nonalcoholic beverages requires management to consider how many varieties to carry; how soft drinks will be dispensed; and who will supply the coffee.

9. Selection factors for purchasing nonalcoholic beverages include:

   - Intended use
   - Exact name
   - U.S. government grades (or equivalent) exist for fruit and vegetable juices; green tea and milk also have grade standards.
   - Brand name (or equivalent)
   - Size of container
   - Type of container
   - Product form—buyers can choose from a variety of pre- and post-mix beverages. Other form considerations include diet or regular colas, coffees, or teas; and grind preferences for coffees.
   - Preservation method
   - AP price
   - Supplier services such as "equipment programs" (in which a supplier gives brewing/dispensing equipment to an operator free or at a greatly reduced price) have made this a crucial decision.

10. The purchasing procedure for nonalcoholic beverages follows a fairly routine pattern.

11. When receiving nonalcoholic beverages, receivers should:

    - Note the effective age of the product, although this is sometimes hard to do with products like coffee.
    - Account for any returned merchandise, including empty returnable containers and kegs.

12. Store nonalcoholic beverages in the correct environment to retard quality deterioration.

13. Managers often do not impose strict controls on the issuing of nonalcoholic beverages.

    - The cost of controlling exceeds the potential savings.
    - Employees are often permitted to drink these beverages for free or for a modest drink fee, so the threat of pilfering is minimal.
    - Many of these items are exchanged constantly between the bar and the kitchen.

Chapter 24 Exercises

1. Compare and contrast liquor purchasing with food purchasing.

_____

_____

_____

_____

L.O. 24.1

2. Compare and contrast liquor purchasing with nonalcoholic beverage purchasing.

_____

_____

_____

_____

L.O. 24.1

3. Why are brand names the most crucial selection factor with beverage alcohols?

_____

_____

_____

L.O. 24.2

4. As the owner of a new restaurant that is going into an existing space, you need to sit down with a contractor to discuss your vision for a new wine cellar to be installed in the current storage facility. What are some of your main concerns with respect to security and proper storage of the wines?

_____

_____

_____

L.O. 24.3

Chapter 24 Check-in

1. Once the decision to sell alcoholic beverages has been made, what is the next step?

   A. Determine the needs of the operation.
   B. Obtain a liquor license.
   C. Decide on the varieties to carry.
   D. Select the quality of liquor to serve.

   L.O. 24.1

2. A customer who asks for Bombay gin has ordered what kind of drink?

   A. Call brand
   B. Well brand
   C. House brand
   D. Premium brand

   L.O. 24.1

3. Which of the following is an indication of alcoholic strength?

   A. Well
   B. Vintage
   C. Draft
   D. Proof

   L.O. 24.1

4. The most fundamental selection factor for alcohol is

   A. brand name.
   B. AP price.
   C. point of origin.
   D. supplier services.

   L.O. 24.2

5. Which of the following nonalcoholic beverages does not have a government grade?

   A. Green tea
   B. Carbonated soda
   C. Milk
   D. Tomato juice

   L.O. 24.2

6. Wines contain approximately how much alcohol?

   A. 3.2% to more than 6%
   B. 12% to 20%
   C. 35% to 75.5%
   D. 80%

   L.O. 24.2

7. Which beverages require reconstitution once they have been bought by a foodservice operation?

   A. Distilled spirits
   B. Postmix products
   C. Tea
   D. Fresh lemonade

   L.O. 24.2

8. Which of the following beverages has the longest shelf life?

   A. Milk
   B. Bottled beer
   C. Distilled spirits
   D. Coffee

   L.O. 24.2

9. The wine expert typically does the
   A. bookkeeping.
   B. buying, receiving, storing, and selling in the dining room.
   C. serving only.
   D. inventory of all costly wine products.

L.O. 24.3

10. Nonalcoholic beverages encourage an operator to follow the
    A. perpetual inventory approach.
    B. allocation approach.
    C. post-off approach.
    D. par stock approach.

L.O. 24.3

CHAPTER 25

NONFOOD EXPENSE ITEMS

Learning Objectives

After reading this chapter, you should be able to:

25.1   Identify management considerations surrounding the selection and procurement of nonfood expense items.

25.2   List the types of nonfood expense items that might be purchased by a hospitality operator.

25.3   Describe the major selection factors for nonfood expense items.

Chapter 25 Study Outline

1. When buying nonfood items, managers must consider the following:

   - Personalization of items such as napkins and matchbooks generally increases the price, but such touches may also enhance the image of the operation with customers.

   - Since product variety and the number of suppliers who carry these items are numerous, the situation favors bid buyers, especially personalized items with varying quality requirements.

   - Degree of product convenience often comes down to a permanent versus disposable decision.

   - Impulse purchasing should be avoided; purchase only nonfood items that are definitely needed.

   - Proper supervision of workers is the key to reducing waste and misuse.

   - Quantity and volume discounts are preferred because they can generate significant savings.

   - Packers' brands are not a prevalent factor in this purchasing category.

   - A **systems sale** occurs when a manufacturer of large-ticket items like a POS system or cash register sells the item at a low price, but recoups this cost over time through subsequent sales of the items needed to run the machine. Buyers should always evaluate the cost of these back-end items before agreeing to a deal.

- Operating supplies schemes—encompassing everything from misleading catalog descriptions to illegal "toner-phoners"—are prevalent within this expense category.

- Safety considerations—concerns about toxic cleaning supplies or pest control cause some buyers to prefer hiring a service to do the work instead.

- New versus used—while tremendous savings can sometimes be had in finding used sources, such efforts take time and involve more risk.

- Equipment programs similar to those for nonalcoholic beverages are often available for items such as dishwashers. While they probably cost more in the long run, such programs free up cash in the short term.

- Lifetime cost—buyers need to consider the operating costs associated with the use of an item—the lifetime cost of a cheaper item might outweigh the greater initial cost of a more expensive, labor-saving device.

- To make sure credit terms are not too beneficial to the supplier, buyers should shop around to get the best deal.

2. Purchasing nonfood items can yield cost-saving opportunities; the major problems are identifying proper par stock and the appropriate supplier.

3. For each typical nonfood item listed below, there are several selection factors to consider.

- **Cleaning supplies**—factors include an item's **as-used cost** (price of item plus cost of labor and energy needed to use it) and its effectiveness, adaptability, safety, ease of use, odor, container size, and supplier services such as product information.

- **Cleaning tools**—factors include its durability, the employee skill required to use it, material used to make the tool, and whether a used tool might do the job just as well.

- **Maintenance supplies**—factors include cost versus expected life of the supply, labor time required, used versus new supplies, and "capitalizing" the expense (buying a new capital item in order to reduce maintenance costs).

- **Permanent ware**—factors include degree of personalization needed and its effect on AP price; the need for different types of permanent ware to look good together; source of supply and its effect on stockless purchase plan options; materials used to make items; sizes; durability versus an item's theft potential; and the possibility of buying used items.

- **Single-service disposable ware**—factors are similar to those surrounding permanent ware, but also may include the degree to which items are recyclable.

- **Preparation and service utensils**—factors are similar to permanent ware, but also include considerations for safety hazards or unusual sanitation difficulties an item might pose, plus a much greater emphasis on the materials used to make an item and their ability to withstand constant wear and tear.

- **Fabrics**—factors include length of service, maintenance schedules, and the impact that the style/choice of fabric may have on the labor costs of maintenance employees or other staff.

- **Other paper products** (guest checks, cash register tape, tissue, etc.)—factors include image; special sizes and other requirements; degree of personalization; the effect of waste on AP price; and minimum-order requirements.
- **Miscellaneous items** (pest control supplies, plant food, etc.)—the biggest factor is deciding whether it is safer and more cost-effective to hire a professional service to handle these dangerous products.

Chapter 25 Exercises

Sophie is the owner/operator of Pasta Prima, a party-themed American-style restaurant that will open in three months.

1. Describe at least three nonfood items that Sophie might want to consider having manufactured with the company's logo on them.

   - _____

   - _____

   - _____

L.O. 25.1

2. Describe the major types of nonfood items that Sophie needs to order before opening day.

   _____

   _____

   _____

   _____

L.O. 25.2

3. According to Pasta Prima's business plan, the take-out portion of the business will eventually be at least twenty-five percent of the overall business. What are some considerations Sophie needs to make before opening the restaurant?

   _____

   _____

   _____

   _____

L.O. 25.3

Chapter 25 Check-in

1. What is the likely effect of the personalization of nonfood items on AP price?

    A. Personalization tends to decrease the AP price.
    B. Personalization tends to increase the AP price.
    C. Personalization has no effect on AP price.
    D. Personalization is a labor issue unrelated to AP price.

    L.O. 25.1

2. The most controversial issue associated with nonfood conveniences centers on

    A. cost savings.
    B. disposable versus reusable items.
    C. perishability.
    D. the negative environmental impact of disposable ware.

    L.O. 25.1

3. Which of the following is not as important for nonfood expense items as it is for food and beverages?

    A. Packers' brands
    B. Cost
    C. Supervision
    D. Product variety

    L.O. 25.1

4. Bleach, soaps, and polishes fall into which nonfood expense category?

    A. Maintenance supplies
    B. Other paper products
    C. Cleaning supplies
    D. Cleaning tools

    L.O. 25.2

5. A buyer would most likely look for high quality materials that are extremely durable, even if the quality translated into a higher price, for which types of items?

    A. Maintenance supplies
    B. Permanent ware
    C. Fabrics
    D. Cleaning tools

    L.O. 25.1

6. For most repair and maintenance needs, hospitality operations contact a

    A. professional service.
    B. handyman.
    C. subcontractor.
    D. scheduling firm.

    L.O. 25.3

7. When buying permanent ware, there is a trade-off between price and

    A. product size.
    B. durability.
    C. effectiveness.
    D. ease of use.

    L.O. 25.2 and 25.3

8. A buyer's initial purchase of preparation and service utensils is treated as a

    A. current expense.
    B. systems sale.
    C. lifetime cost.
    D. capital investment.

    L.O. 25.2

9. Which of the following is a selection factor when purchasing fabrics?

   A. Cost
   B. Adaptability
   C. Maintenance
   D. Odor

   L.O. 25.3

10. Since other paper products are often significantly wasted in usage, which of the following selection factors is vital when purchasing them?

    A. AP price
    B. Length of service
    C. Packaging
    D. Size

    L.O. 25.3

CHAPTER 26

Learning Objectives

After reading this chapter, you should be able to:

26.1   Identify management considerations surrounding the selection and procurement of services.

26.2   List the types of services that might be purchased by a hospitality operator.

26.3   Outline the general procedures used when purchasing services.

26.4   Describe the major selection factors for services.

Chapter 26 Study Outline

1. When purchasing services, managers must consider the following factors:

    *   Not all services are fixed costs; time and effort should be spent purchasing them.

    *   It can be difficult to evaluate a service provider's performance.

    *   An operation must decide whether to provide its own service or to buy it.

    *   It is necessary to examine a service provider's background and abilities.

    *   An operator must consider the advantages and disadvantages of using moonlighters.

2. When purchasing a service, complete specs are essential for bid buying.

    *   Often the best approach is to settle on one service provider (based on current references), then work with that company to determine the services needed, the cost to do those services correctly, and payment arrangements needed to receive those services.

3. For each typical service purchased below, there are several selection factors to consider:

    *   **Waste removal**—factors include the provider's ability to provide on-time collection; to take care with the containers and housing area; to remove refuse piled on the ground; to return containers to their proper location; to equip operation with suitable containers and locks if necessary; and to do this at a competitive price.

    *   **Financial** (e.g., banks)—buyers look for the range of services that a bank can provide, from checking and payroll accounts to loan capital.

142

- **Groundskeeping** (landscaping, snow removal, parking lot maintenance, etc.)—while some services are often provided by landlord via a **common area maintenance (CAM) fee**, selection factors include ensuring the provider has a demonstrated knowledge of the trade(s) and developing specific specs of the services desired.

- **Pest control**—factors include rate of regular visits; price for emergency infestations; and overall expertise on methods to reduce pest-infestation problems.

- **Advertising**—factors include deciding which media to advertise in, such as newspapers, radio, television, Web sites, magazines, telephone directories, print materials, outdoor signs, and direct-mail; appropriate cost per potential customer reached; the degree to which an operation wants to be identified with a supplier who is willing to pay for menu printing and sign-preparation costs; support of athletic teams and other community relationships; and the various payment options common to advertising agencies and media-buying services.

- **Consulting** (designers, lawyers, accountants, bookkeepers, employee trainers, computer specialists, etc.)—factors include using consultant's proposals as a means of better defining the service needed; negotiating fixed-fee contracts instead of open-ended contracts (which tend to invite overbilling); balancing fees with desire to have the service completed satisfactorily; and the possibility of receiving some consulting services for free.

- **Decorating and remodeling**—factors include making sure a contractor is licensed, insured, and large enough to do the job professionally, on time, and at the agreed-upon budget; seeing examples of the contractors' previous work; negotiating performance bonds to ensure work is completed; and avoiding lien-sale contracts by paying in installments and requiring contractors to sign unconditional lien releases upon final payment.

- **Maintenance** (security, fire alarms, locksmith, refrigeration, window-washing, etc.)—factors include understanding the difference between service and maintenance agreements; paying up front for service to be rendered; and making sure services are available as advertised.

- **Vending machine**—factors include which, if any, machines are needed; quality differences among different machines; commission splits between the vendor and the operation; whether the operation should buy the machine outright; and national vending machine programs available for large, multiunit operations.

- **Insurance**—operators protect themselves with a wide variety of insurance policies. Factors to be considered include the extent of coverage, amount of deductible to be paid, exclusions to the policy, and what conditions must be met in order for the operation to collect.

- **Laundry and linen supply**—factors include what degree of service is most appropriate; whether using disposable linens and giving employees a uniform fee is more cost-effective; length of contract; service schedule; provisions for seasonal fluctuations; and cost of service and lost goods.

- **Cleaning**—factors include which services may be better handled by employees themselves; competitive pricing due to the large number of providers available; and the tendency for operators to be lax when inspecting the services that have been performed.

4. Security measures for purchasing services include checking all invoices carefully and being wary of contractors who demand a deposit before beginning work.

Chapter 26 Exercises

1. What management considerations and/or problems are associated with buying services?

_____

_____

_____

L.O. 26.1

2. Name three selection factors for each service below.
   a. Waste removal
   - _____

   - _____

   - _____

   b. Vending machines
   - _____

   - _____

   - _____

   c. Insurance
   - _____

   - _____

   - _____

L.O. 26.4

3. On a separate piece of paper, write a spec for one of the following: financial services, groundskeeping, pest control, or advertising.

L.O. 26.3

Chapter 26 Check-in

1. When is an operator able to judge the quality of a service?

   A. When the work is finished
   B. When the work has begun
   C. After interviewing the service provider
   D. After talking to the references supplied by the service provider

L.O. 26.1

2. Contracting with a service provider to do work that is not central to the hospitality company's primary mission is called

   A. bonding.
   B. moonlighting.
   C. outsourcing.
   D. outlying.

L.O. 26.1

3. Which of the following is used by a landlord to defray the costs of parking lot maintenance, window cleaning, waste removal, and other expenses related to the general upkeep of common areas?

   A. Due bill
   B. CAM fee
   C. Lien
   D. Trade out

L.O. 26.1

4. Which of the following is not easy to detail on a specification for services?

   A. Inspection procedures
   B. Objectives to be accomplished
   C. Completion date
   D. Price

L.O. 26.3

5. The only relevant aspect of service purchasing is to

   A. hire only the most reputable service providers.
   B. pay as low a price as possible.
   C. eliminate the need to monitor the actual work.
   D. get what you want.

L.O. 26.3

6. The most difficult groundskeeping service to purchase is the

   A. snow-removal service.
   B. landscaping service.
   C. parking lot maintenance service.
   D. waste-removal service.

L.O. 26.2

7. When purchasing pest-control services, the best strategy is to

   A. contract for a weekly or monthly visit.
   B. call only when an obvious problem arises.
   C. contract for emergency service.
   D. hire a firm on retainer.

L.O. 26.2, 26.4

8. Which advertising medium tends to build business slowly over the long run?

   A. Outdoor ads
   B. Television
   C. Radio
   D. Internet

   L.O. 26.2, 26.4

9. For which of the following would an operator tend to hire a consultant?

   A. Menu design
   B. Creation of feasibility studies
   C. Hiring wait staff
   D. Accounting and bookkeeping

   L.O. 26.2, 26.4

10. Which of the following covers equipment defects and malfunctions during the warranty period?

    A. Service agreement
    B. Maintenance contract
    C. Extended policies
    D. Risk plan

    L.O. 26.2, 26.4

CHAPTER 27

FURNITURE, FIXTURES, AND EQUIPMENT

Learning Objectives

After reading this chapter, you should be able to:

27.1   Identify management considerations surrounding the selection and procurement of furniture, fixtures, and equipment.

27.2   Outline the general procedures used when purchasing furniture, fixtures, and equipment.

27.3   Describe the major selection factors for furniture, fixtures, and equipment.

27.4   Explain methods to finance the purchase of furniture, fixtures, and equipment.

Chapter 27 Study Outline

1. Furniture, fixtures, and equipment (FFE) are sometimes referred to as capital items, since their value is depreciated over a period of years.

2. Before purchasing FFE, a manager/buyer should consider the following:
   - How does the operation's future plans impact today's FFE needs?
   - At what point does capitalizing operating expenses by purchasing higher-quality equipment become economically advisable? (In general, operational savings should offset the original investment within two to three years.)
   - Who should select and procure the FFE items—users, owner/managers, buyers, or consultants?
   - Will the efficiencies that consultants often add to an operation's design offset their fees?
   - Which type of FFE supply source should an operation choose?
   - Could reconditioning/remodeling some items instead of replacing them be more cost effective?

3. General procedures for FFE purchases include:
   - Visiting trade shows to consider several FFE items and potential suppliers.
   - Since most FFE purchases are financed through a lender, competitive bids are often required as part of the loan process.

- FFE purchase specifications will usually include instructions to bidders, general and specific conditions, and detailed drawings.
- Developing an approved-supplier list and select the best supplier
- Modify specifications if necessary, monitor FFE orders and delivery, oversee any necessary subcontracting, and obtain training and other start-up help as needed.

4. Selection factors for purchasing FFE items include:

- Intended use
- Exact name, including specific types of equipment and model numbers.
- Lifetime cost—besides the AP price, operators must consider trade-in value of the old FFE item; delivery, installation, and testing costs for the new FFE item; relevant operating costs; potential operating savings; and anticipated eventual trade-in value of the new FFE item.
- Potential operating savings to the cost of merchandise, labor, energy, taxes, water, waste removal, or other operating expenses often serve as major incentives to purchase new FFE items. Still, operators must be careful when suppliers cite greater productivity or product savings as major reasons for buying an item, as such savings are often illusory.
- Direct purchases may lower the AP price on a FFE item, but the cost of transportation, installation, maintenance, and other supplier services may make the local dealer's markup a better value in the long run.
- Demonstration models are cheaper, but operators usually have to pay for the item all at once in cash, take the item as is, and provide their own transportation/installation.
- Equipment programs on FFE items have generally been advantageous to hospitality operators.
- Custom FFE items are expensive both in their initial AP prices and in their potential lifetime costs; still, if these items provide the operation with exactly what it needs, they can be very economical.
- New versus used FFE: operators can save as much as seventy percent of new AP prices, often for goods that have suffered little or no use. Still, used FFE items take time to find and are often obsolete, energy-inefficient, inappropriate in size, and expensive to maintain.
- Versatility in equipment can often reduce the size of the production facilities while increasing the amount of income-producing area. Compactness in equipment can achieve a similar space savings.
- Compatibility of the new item with existing FFE items, both aesthetically and functionally.
- Appearance of FFE items is crucial in conveying the right image of the operation to its customers.

- Brand name, and the "halo effect" that a brand often generates, is the selection factor used almost exclusively by most operators when purchasing replacement FFE.
- Portability of an FFE item has many advantages: it can be used for off-site banquets or events, it is easier to maintain and repair, and it often retains its value over the long run.
- Ease of cleaning—good quality items often take less time to clean, last longer, and are less likely to harbor bacteria, pests, or dirt.
- Ease of maintenance is often worth a slightly higher initial AP price.
- Degree of automation in an FFE item should be seen in terms of the amount of quality control or cost-control efforts that it can provide.
- Concerns about the availability of replacement parts and potential time lags in getting them are magnified with the purchase of used, technologically unique, or custom equipment.
- Supplier services, specifically "service after the sale," is the most important concern for operators when selecting a supplier.
- Employee skill level and potential resistance to change are both factors that can impact the acceptance of a new FFE item.
- Source of energy—when a choice exists for a type of equipment, operators look for a less expensive energy source or one that is least damaging to the environment.
- Excess capacity—operators need to decide whether to buy for today's or tomorrow's customer load.
- Add-on capabilities—FFE items that are modular in design can be easily adapted to service additional business.
- Warranties on FFE items typically cover parts and repair for one to two years from date of shipment. Operators should make sure warranties begin once an item is put into service.
- Code compliance of local fire, health, safety, and building procedures is a must with FFE items; several organizations provide certification of an item's compliance, which is typically denoted by a seal of approval.

5. To purchase FFE items, operators usually make a down payment in cash, followed by arranging a variety of credit options, including promissory notes, installment payment plans, credit cards, loans from commercial lenders, or leasing arrangements.
   - Operators often devote as much time to the financing of FFE items as they do to selecting them.

Chapter 27 Exercises

1. What is a depreciable asset?

_____

_____

_____

L.O. 27.1

2. How does the life expectancy of an FFE item affect the purchase of FFEs?

_____

_____

_____

L.O. 27.1

3. How do future plans enter into the FFE purchasing decision?

_____

_____

_____

L.O. 27.1

4. List the expenses and considerations associated with an FFE item it over its normal life span in addition to its initial AP price.

_____

_____

_____

L.O. 27.1

5. Describe the payback period formula and the net present value procedure.

_____

_____

_____

L.O. 27.2

6. What is the "halo effect? "

_____

_____

_____

L.O. 27.3

7. What are some of the considerations that should go into evaluating the potential savings of automated equipment?

_____

_____

_____

L.O. 27.3

8. Why might an operator be inclined to buy kitchen equipment that handles only the current customer load? Conversely, why might the operator decide to purchase excess-capacity equipment now?

_____

_____

_____

L.O. 27.3

9. Name three ways to finance an FFE purchase.

• _____

• _____

• _____

L.O. 27.4

Chapter 27 Check-in

1. By investing today in an expensive piece of machinery that will ultimately reduce energy consumption, an operator is doing which of the following?

   A. Depreciating an asset
   B. Capitalizing an operating expense
   C. Financing the purchase of FFE
   D. Trading in

   L.O. 27.1

2. The final decision regarding any FFE purchase belongs to the

   A. user.
   B. buyer.
   C. consultant.
   D. owner/manager.

   L.O. 27.1

3. What is the best way for hospitality operators to examine replacement FFE before making their purchase decisions?

   A. Attending trade shows
   B. Visiting dealer showrooms
   C. Hosting an FFE "event"
   D. Looking through catalogs

   L.O. 27.2

4. What is typically included in a specification for an FFE item that is not included in a specification for other items?

   A. Instructions to bidders
   B. Treatment of delays
   C. Detailed drawings
   D. Delivery dates

   L.O. 27.2

5. Which of the following is difficult to achieve in the hospitality industry?

   A. Code compliance
   B. Labor saving
   C. Automation
   D. Excess capacity

   L.O. 27.3

6. The amount of time it takes to recoup the original investment is called the

   A. payback period.
   B. installation period.
   C. finance period.
   D. warranty period.

   L.O. 27.3

7. What is the major potential advantage of used merchandise?

   A. Replacement part availability
   B. Huge reduction in the purchase price
   C. Long, useful life
   D. Energy efficiency

   L.O. 27.3

8. Since the cost of space in the hospitality operation is very expensive, which of the following is increasingly important when purchasing FFE?

   A. Equipment programs
   B. Compatibility
   C. Appearance
   D. Versatility

   L.O. 27.3

9. Which selection factor is used almost exclusively to purchase replacement FFE?

    A. Compactness
    B. Lifetime cost
    C. Brand name
    D. Portability

L.O. 27.3

10. Operators who arrange an installment-payment plan with a dealer are usually expected to

    A. make weekly payments.
    B. pay for forty-eight to sixty months.
    C. make a down payment of one-third the purchase price of the item.
    D. have an impeccable credit record.

L.O. 27.4

Practice Test

1. Which of the following statements best describes the difference between the terms "procurement" and "purchasing"?

   A. "Procurement" is a broad term that describes all of the functions involved in selecting, buying, receiving, and storing supplies, while "purchasing" is a limited term describing the ordering and paying for goods.

   B. "Procurement" is a formal term that describes the ethical and legal functions of the purchaser, while "purchasing" is an informal term used frequently by those in the foodservice industry.

   C. "Procurement" is the term used to describe the purchasing function within large multiunit companies and hotels, while "purchasing" is the term used to describe the purchasing function within smaller chains and independent operations.

   D. "Procurement" is a theoretical term used in the academic world, while "purchasing" is the term commonly used within the foodservice industry.

   L.O. 1.1

2. Which of the following foodservice operations is considered part of the noncommercial industry segment?

   A. Food court
   B. Independently owned restaurant
   C. Resort
   D. Hospital foodservice

   L.O. 1.2

3. In which type of system do hospitality operations come together to achieve savings by purchasing food and supplies in bulk?

   A. Co-op
   B. E-marketplace
   C. B2B
   D. E-procurement

   L.O. 1.2

4. Which of the following allows users to delete menu items, track employee activity, analyze worker productivity, and force-order modifiers?

   A. Fax machines
   B. Personal computers
   C. Computerized POS systems
   D. Bar-code readers

   L.O. 2.1

5. Employees may resist incorporating e-procurement strategies for all of the following reasons except

   A. their sense that technology is evolving too quickly.
   B. they fear giving up the power that knowledge of the old system gives them.
   C. they suspect that learning a new work routine may hurt their job performance.
   D. they fear disintermediation with their suppliers.

   L.O. 2.2

6. In the future, which of the following will distinguish one supplier from another?

   A. Product lines
   B. Technology used
   C. Product prices
   D. Warehouse locations

   L.O. 2.1

7. Which of the following is *not* considered an intermediary?

   A. Distributor
   B. Grower
   C. Commissary
   D. Wholesale club

   L.O. 3.1

8. From the standpoint of maximizing an operation's optimal value, why might a buyer for a vegetarian restaurant decide to pay more for produce that is delivered daily rather than twice a week?

   A. Superior supplier services rarely add much value to an operation.
   B. Optimal value can be derived only when there are few supplier services included.
   C. Suppliers are able to charge less for daily deliveries and pass these savings onto their customers.
   D. Not having to worry about produce stockouts allows management to focus more on their customers.

   L.O. 3.3

9. As an item travels through the distribution channel, what is most likely to happen?

   A. Value will increase as it is altered for consumption.
   B. Quality will improve as it is processed.
   C. Price will increase as costs are added.
   D. Flavor will be enhanced as it is processed.

   L.O. 3.2

10. Prices for products in their initial stages of production are often set through

   A. Bidding procedure.
   B. product differentiation.
   C. perceived value.
   D. EP costing.

   L.O. 4.1

11. A Packed Under Federal Inspection (PUFI) seal can be found on what type of food item?

   A. Fresh produce
   B. Cheese
   C. Fish
   D. Meat

   L.O. 4.3

12. Which of the following constitutes a form of product preservation?

   A. Genetic engineering
   B. Transportation
   C. Computerization
   D. Advertising and promotion

   L.O. 4.4

13. "Sourcing" between a buyer and a supplier is usually
    A. beneficial to both the buyer, who gains a reliable source, and the supplier, who enjoys a steady flow of business.
    B. considered unethical because it can lead to irrelevant considerations on purchasing decisions.
    C. engaged in almost all countries except the U.S.
    D. sought by buyers but not suppliers.
L.O. 5.1

14. A buyer who evaluates whether or not an operation should prepare an item in-house or buy a premade or value-added product is performing
    A. outsourcing.
    B. make-or-buy analysis.
    C. value analysis.
    D. yield analysis.
L.O. 5.2

15. Which of the following is not one of the main objectives of the purchasing function?
    A. Maintain adequate supply of product and services.
    B. Minimize investments yet avoid stockouts between deliveries.
    C. Maintain product quality by requiring consistency of products and services over time.
    D. Maintain a competitive position by driving down AP prices all the time.
L.O. 5.3

16. Multiunit chains generally are organized for purchasing differently from independent operations because they
    A. assign several different managers per unit to perform purchasing functions.
    B. have an additional level of management.
    C. tend to have simpler and more streamlined purchasing processes.
    D. have a need for higher-quality products.
L.O. 6.1

17. A direct control system, in which the general manager or operator maintains strict control of all purchasing activities, is most likely to be found in which of the following operations?
    A. Food and beverage department of a large urban hotel
    B. Large, multiunit restaurant chain
    C. Small, independently owned restaurant
    D. Food and beverage operations of a concert and events arena.
L.O. 6.2

18. Which of the following lists the qualities sought in a job candidate?
    A. Job specification
    B. Job description
    C. Compensation package
    D. Budget
L.O. 7.3

19. Steward sales occur whenever a hospitality company allows its employees to

A. take advantage of the company's purchasing power to purchase goods for their own private use.
B. enjoy free samples provided by suppliers.
C. purchase company stock.
D. use excess food products for their own personal gatherings.

L.O. 7.2

20. A full-service restaurant with an annual sales volume of $2,000,000 should have an inventory of food, beverage, and nonfood supplies that is equal in dollar value to no more than

A. $2,000.
B. $20,000.
C. $50,000.
D. $40,000.

L.O. 7.2

21. Compared to product specifications, purchase specifications contain

A. legal language.
B. additional information.
C. the signature of the supplier.
D. fewer product details.

L.O. 8.1

22. The lower the skill level of employees, the more buyers must rely on

A. purchase specifications.
B. multiple bidders.
C. credit terms.
D. portion-controlled food.

L.O. 8.3

23. If delivery requirements and quality-tolerance limits are unreasonable, they usually add to the

A. overall value.
B. AP price.
C. EP price.
D. need for periodic revision.

L.O. 8.3

24. A level of inventory that a buyer determines must be on hand to maintain a continuing supply of each item from one delivery date to the next is called the

A. reorder point.
B. correct order size.
C. par stock.
D. popularity index.

L.O. 9.1

25. Order size stays the same but order time varies with the use of which approach?

A. Theoretical
B. Levinson
C. Par stock
D. EOQ

L.O. 9.2

26. If an operation qualifies for only once-a-week delivery, a buyer will have a difficult time trying to implement

A. the par stock approach.
B. the EOQ and ROP concepts.
C. just-in-time inventory management programs.
D. the Levinson approach.

L.O. 9.2

27. A buyer who requests an itemized bill is almost always

    A. an accountant.
    B. price conscious.
    C. the operation's owner/manager.
    D. concerned with supplier services.

L.O. 10.1

28. In cost-plus purchasing, the price of an item is based on

    A. supply and demand considerations.
    B. estimates of what the item will cost in the near future.
    C. the supplier's cost plus a markup set by the supplier and buyer.
    D. competitive forces.

L.O. 10.2 & 10.3

29. A restaurant that gets its linens at cost from a supplier who holds meetings there once a month at a reduced rate is engaging in

    A. co-op buying.
    B. stockless purchasing.
    C. hedging.
    D. exchange bartering.

L.O. 10.3

30. Which of the following is a sound principle of cash management?

    A. Pay all bills early.
    B. Put off collecting money due as long as possible.
    C. Keep cash transactions to a minimum.
    D. Keep your money as long as possible.

L.O. 11.1

31. Which of the following is likely to limit an operator's ability to invest?

    A. Collecting bills due sooner than necessary
    B. Paying bills sooner than necessary
    C. Paying bills too late
    D. Collecting bills without invoicing them

L.O. 11.2

32. A fixed bid is likely to be used, rather than a daily bid, for which of the following items?

    A. Paper cocktail napkins, matchbooks, and cocktail straws ordered every three months
    B. Fresh produce ordered twice weekly
    C. Ice cream and frozen desserts ordered weekly
    D. Fresh fish ordered daily

L.O. 12.1

33. The primary appeal to buyers of one-stop shopping is

    A. convenience.
    B. low prices.
    C. optimal supplier services.
    D. high quality.

L.O. 12.2

34. The major characteristics of an operation's buying behavior is often kept in the supplier's

    A. requests for bid.
    B. value analysis.
    C. buyer profiles.
    D. long-term contracts.

L.O. 12.3

35. Purchase requisitions typically are prepared by

    A. the buyer and given to a supplier.
    B. department heads and given to the buyer.
    C. a supplier and given to prospective buyers.
    D. a supplier and given to regular buyers.

L.O. 13.1

36. The typical purchase order resembles the

    A. back order.
    B. market quote.
    C. product requisition.
    D. purchase requisition.

L.O. 13.2

37. Which of the following can streamline the ordering procedure?

    A. Expediting
    B. Suppliers' forms
    C. Change orders
    D. Levinson approach

L.O. 13.3

38. To avoid rushing the receiver, deliveries should be

    A. scheduled for arrival at the end of the day.
    B. staggered.
    C. made first thing in the morning.
    D. accompanied by a copy of all specifications and the purchase order.

L.O. 14.2

39. What is the most difficult kind of check that a receiving clerk can make?

    A. Quantity check
    B. Price check
    C. Quality check
    D. Package check

L.O. 14.3

40. Which of the following food items is sometimes tagged to ensure proper control?

    A. Dairy products
    B. Meat
    C. Fish
    D. Canned items

L.O. 14.4

41. Which of the following is a form of pilferage?

    A. Premeditated burglary
    B. Eating on the job
    C. Improper stock rotation
    D. Spoilage

L.O. 15.1

42. Which of the following should be stored at 32°F to 40°F?

    A. Fish
    B. Live shellfish
    C. Dairy products
    D. Meat and poultry

L.O. 15.2

43. Which of the following tasks is most often assigned to a receiver-storeroom manager?

    A. Disposing of items that are no longer used by the operation

    B. Issuing items needed by various departments in the operation

    C. Conducting performance appraisals of production personnel

    D. Calculating product costs

L.O. 15.3

44. Restricting access to all receiving and storage areas can easily prevent which of the following security problems?

    A. Inventory padding

    B. Inventory theft

    C. Kickbacks

    D. Spoilers

L.O. 16.1

45. Which of the following hospitality employees are typically bonded?

    A. Servers

    B. Front-desk personnel

    C. Cashiers

    D. Managers

L.O. 16.2

46. What is the one crucial factor in control and security that is often omitted?

    A. Employee supervision

    B. Checks and balances

    C. Alarm systems

    D. Critical-item inventory analysis

L.O. 16.2

47. When a manager or operator writes specs calling for Sunkist oranges, she is using a

    A. packer's brand.

    B. U.S. quality grade.

    C. lug.

    D. product yield.

L.O. 17.1

48. Which of the following prevents moisture loss and contributes to the appearance of some produce items?

    A. U.S. grading

    B. Layering

    C. Ripening

    D. Waxing

L.O. 17.1

49. The first step in purchasing fresh produce is to

    A. decide on the exact type of product and quality desired.

    B. prepare specifications for each item.

    C. obtain *The Produce Marketing Association Fresh Produce Reference Manual for Food Service.*

    D. consider the suppliers likely to satisfy the operation's needs.

L.O. 17.2

50. Food items that are pickled or fermented are purchased almost exclusively for

    A. convenience.

    B. AP price considerations.

    C. the taste the processing imparts.

    D. the longer shelf life that results from the processing.

L.O. 18.1

51. The term "heavy pack" on a canned food product means that
    A. a product's container weighs more than the product itself.
    B. a lot of juice has been added.
    C. no juice has been added.
    D. some juice has been added, but not much.

L.O. 18.2

52. If competing salespeople or suppliers are present when an operator is performing a can-cutting test, the testing is referred to as
    A. holding court.
    B. forward buying.
    C. impulse purchasing.
    D. wholesale testing.

L.O. 18.3

53. The highest grade of fluid milk is
    A. A.
    B. AA.
    C. Fancy.
    D. Premium.

L.O. 19.1

54. Government inspection of dairy processing methods ensures which of the following?
    A. Wholesomeness
    B. Flavor
    C. Convenience
    D. Packaging

L.O. 19.1

55. Which dairy products should be issued first?
    A. Milk
    B. Those requiring refrigeration
    C. Older products
    D. Those containing a high concentration of butterfat

L.O. 19.2

56. The highest grade given to fresh shell eggs is
    A. AA.
    B. A.
    C. Prime.
    D. Choice.

L.O. 20.1

57. Eggs preserved under which method are not sold to foodservice operators?
    A. Overwrapping
    B. Oil dipping
    C. Oil spraying
    D. Controlled-atmosphere storage

L.O. 20.1

58. The biggest challenge in selecting a fresh egg supplier is
    A. choosing from among a limited number of purveyors.
    B. determining which supplier provides the freshest eggs.
    C. deciding upon a mutually beneficial AP price.
    D. agreeing on an acceptable delivery schedule.

L.O. 20.2

59. A characteristic of both free-range and kosher chickens is that they have been

   A. processed before shipping.
   B. frozen during shipping.
   C. slaughtered before eight weeks old.
   D. allowed to roam free before slaughter.

L.O. 21.1

60. Storing poultry in ice generally

   A. causes it to discolor.
   B. leads to faster spoilage.
   C. extends its shelf life.
   D. causes it to lose flavor.

L.O. 21.2

61. The USDA's Acceptance Service allows an operator to

   A. streamline the poultry receiving process.
   B. determine proper poultry storage temperatures.
   C. track in-process inventories of poultry.
   D. evaluate potential poultry suppliers.

L.O. 21.2

62. When fish carries a PUFI seal, it means that the product

   A. was produced in an establishment that meets federal sanitary guidelines.
   B. has been visually inspected by a government agent.
   C. comes from a government-approved aquaculture site.
   D. is less than three days old.

L.O. 22.1

63. Packing fish in modified atmosphere packaging (MAP)

   A. is less expensive than ice packing.
   B. is easier to receive than conventional packaging.
   C. extends the shelf life of the fish.
   D. allows the buyer to see the product inside.

L.O. 22.2

64. Which of the following is a sign that a shipment of fish is fresh and acceptable to receive?

   A. Soft flesh
   B. Fishy scent
   C. Gray gills
   D. Clear, bright eyes

L.O. 22.2

65. A key factor in choosing the type and amount of processing for fresh meat items is the

   A. quality desired.
   B. IMPS number.
   C. AP price.
   D. product yield.

L.O. 23.1

66. Which of the following is considered a variety meat?

   A. Sausage
   B. Veal
   C. Venison
   D. Pheasant

L.O. 23.2

67. Which of the following is the highest USDA grade given to beef?

A. Select
B. Prime
C. Choice
D. No. 1

L.O. 23.2

68. An operator who wants to pay a meat expert to write meat specifications and to ensure that the specified products are actually delivered can use which of the following?

A. Product Examination Service
B. Certified Buying Service
C. MBG Number Service
D. USDA's Acceptance Service

L.O. 23.3

69. You would expect to see private, exclusive distributorships in which one of the following product categories?

A. Beverage alcohol
B. Produce
C. Hospitality furnishings
D. Poultry

L.O. 24.1

70. Liquor that is 100 proof contains what percentage of alcohol?

A. 10%
B. 50%
C. 100%
D. 200%

L.O. 24.2

71. When purchasing soft drinks, which of the following is typical?

A. Day-to-day standing order
B. Three-day stock
C. One-week stock
D. Monthly stock

L.O. 24.3

72. Whenever possible, an operator should purchase nonfood items

A. by packer's brand.
B. in large amounts.
C. from primarily one supplier.
D. in a used condition.

L.O. 25.1

73. A buyer can procure which of the following by buying, leasing, or using disposables?

A. Permanent ware
B. Cleaning tools
C. Fabrics
D. Paper products

L.O. 25.2 and 25.3

74. Packaging is a selection factor associated with which category of nonfood item?

A. Single-service disposable ware
B. Cleaning supplies
C. Maintenance supplies
D. Permanent ware

L.O. 25.3

75. One of the main things to remember about services is that they are

A. unavoidable costs of doing business.
B. easy to monitor and inspect.
C. not frequently outsourced.
D. not all fixed costs.

L.O. 26.1

76. Consultants who focus on the severity of the problem and the obstacles of its solution are engaging in

 A. direct consulting.
 B. negative selling.
 C. PCO.
 D. bantering.

L.O. 26.2

77. The conditions that must be satisfied before an operator can collect are a major selection factor when purchasing

 A. insurance.
 B. financial services.
 C. consulting services.
 D. decorating and remodeling services.

L.O. 26.4

78. The owner/manager is more actively involved in the purchase of which of the following than the purchase of any other product?

 A. Liquor
 B. Meat
 C. FFE
 D. Services

L.O. 27.1

79. Some managers and operators buy demonstration models of FFE because the models are

 A. sturdier than regular models.
 B. more attractive than regular models.
 C. sold at significant cost savings.
 D. designed especially for their operations.

L.O. 27.3

80. Which of the following is the least expensive form of financing FFE items?

 A. Using a credit card
 B. Leasing
 C. Obtaining a loan from a commercial lender
 D. Arranging an installment-payment plan with a dealer

L.O. 27.4

Practice Test Answer Key

1.	B	pp. 1–2	28.	C	p. 217	55.	C	p. 452
2.	D	p. 5	29.	D	pp. 218–219	56.	A	p. 460
3.	A	p. 7	30.	D	p. 239	57.	D	p. 466
4.	C	p. 15	31.	B	p. 240	58.	B	p. 467
5.	D	pp. 31–32	32.	A	p. 251	59.	D	p. 479
6.	B	p. 34	33.	A	p. 253	60.	C	p. 482
7.	B	pp. 49–52	34.	C	p. 270	61.	A	p. 490
8.	D	p. 64	35.	B	p. 282	62.	A	p. 502
9.	C	p. 61	36.	D	p. 285	63.	C	p. 505
10.	A	p. 70	37.	B	pp. 291–292	64.	D	p. 513
11.	C	p. 78	38.	B	p. 302	65.	C	pp. 522–523
12.	B	p. 89	39.	C	p. 305	66.	A	p. 530
13.	A	pp. 100–101	40.	B	p. 314	67.	B	p. 536
14.	B	p. 103	41.	B	p. 328	68.	D	p. 546
15.	D	pp. 108–109	42.	D	p. 332	69.	A	p. 564
16.	B	p. 121	43.	A	p. 337	70.	B	p. 567
17.	C	p. 118	44.	B	p. 355	71.	B	p. 593
18.	A	p. 130	45.	C	p. 361	72.	B	p. 601
19.	A	p. 135	46.	A	p. 367	73.	C	p. 618
20.	B	p. 141	47.	A	p. 379	74.	A	p. 616
21.	B	p. 149	48.	D	p. 386	75.	D	p. 625
22.	D	p. 158	49.	C	p. 387	76.	B	p. 643
23.	B	p. 162	50.	C	p. 405	77.	A	pp. 648–649
24.	C	p. 179	51.	D	p. 418	78.	C	p. 659
25.	A	p. 191	52.	A	p. 425	79.	C	p. 671
26.	B	p. 195	53.	A	p. 440	80.	D	pp. 686–687
27.	B	p. 206	54.	A	p. 447			

Chapter Check-in Answer Key

Chapter 1
1. B   p. 1
2. C   p. 1
3. C   p. 6
4. A   pp. 2–3
5. D   p. 5
6. C   p. 4
7. A   p. 4
8. D   p. 5
9. A   p. 7
10. B   p. 7

Chapter 2
1. C   p. 13
2. A   pp. 12–13
3. D   p. 13
4. B   p. 15
5. D   pp. 15–17
6. B   p. 22
7. A   p. 22
8. C   p. 26
9. B   pp. 30–31
10. C   p. 28

Chapter 3
1. B   p. 48
2. B   p. 49
3. C   pp. 49–52
4. A   p. 49
5. D   p. 58
6. C   p. 59
7. B   p. 58
8. C   p. 59
9. A   pp. 61–62
10. C   p. 62

Chapter 4
1. A   p. 70
2. B   p. 72
3. C   p. 73
4. C   p. 74
5. D   p. 75
6. C   p. 78
7. D   p. 81
8. A   p. 85
9. B   pp. 86–87
10. A   p. 90

Chapter 5
1. A   p. 100
2. A   p. 100
3. C   p. 101
4. A   p. 102
5. C   p. 103
6. B   p. 102
7. B   p. 104
8. D   p. 108
9. A   p. 109
10. D   p. 110

Chapter 6
1. B   p. 118
2. B   p. 118
3. A   p. 118
4. A   p. 119
5. B   p. 120
6. C   p. 122
7. C   p. 123
8. C   p. 123
9. C   p. 124
10. D   p. 124

Chapter 7
1. C   p. 130
2. C   p. 133
3. A   p. 134
4. D   p. 136
5. B   p. 137
6. A   p. 139
7. D   pp. 139–142
8. D   p. 140
9. A   p. 138
10. D   p. 145

Chapter 8
1. A   p. 149
2. B   p. 152
3. C   p. 154
4. D   p. 158
5. D   p. 160
6. C   p. 162
7. B   p. 162
8. A   p. 166
9. B   p. 168
10. C   p. 169

Chapter 9
1. A   p. 178
2. C   p. 179
3. C   p. 179
4. B   p. 182
5. D   p. 182
6. D   pp. 182–184
7. B   p. 187
8. B   p. 188
9. A   pp. 193–194
10. B   p. 196